Kaleidoscope

10 Dynamic Quilt Designs

Paper Piecing

Nancy Mahoney

Martingale®
& COMPANY

Kaleidoscope Paper Piecing:
10 Dynamic Quilt Designs
© 2012 by Nancy Mahoney

That Patchwork Place® is an
imprint of Martingale & Company®.

Martingale & Company
19021 120th Ave. NE, Suite 102
Bothell, WA 98011-9511 USA
www.martingale-pub.com

Printed in China

17 16 15 14 13 12   8 7 6 5 4 3 2 1

Library of Congress
Cataloging-in-Publication Data
is available upon request.

ISBN: 978-1-60468-062-1

Mission Statement

Dedicated to providing quality products and service to inspire creativity.

Credits

President & CEO: Tom Wierzbicki

Editor in Chief: Mary V. Green

Design Director: Paula Schlosser

Managing Editor: Karen Costello Soltys

Technical Editor: Laurie Baker

Copy Editor: Melissa Bryan

Production Manager: Regina Girard

Cover & Text Designer: Regina Girard

Illustrator: Adrienne Smitke

Photographer: Brent Kane

Contents

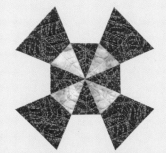

Introduction

I'm often asked how I come up with ideas for my quilt designs. Sometimes it happens in a reverse sort of way; I design a quilt that will showcase a specific fabric collection. I think about the fabrics and formulate a few ideas of how I think the fabric will look in a finished quilt. Then I tweak the design a little and everything falls into place to create a stunning design. OK, it's not really that simple, but that's how I'd like to think it happens! Actually, there are times when I change the design completely, often more than once, until finally the planets line up and everything truly *does* come together in a stunning design.

Other times, I stumble upon the quilt design first, and then it blooms into an idea for a book. That's what happened with this book. When I began quilting more than 25 years ago, if you wanted to create a quilt design, you started with graph paper, a sharp pencil, an eraser, a ruler, and colored pencils. Then along came computerized quilt-design programs, like Electric Quilt, which I fell in love with right from the beginning; it's so easy to draw blocks and play with designs and fabric choices. One day, I started drawing Kaleidoscope blocks, changing them—adding and subtracting lines—until I had lots of different

blocks. (They're a bit like chocolates—I always want one more!) Then I'd play with the blocks until I had a few quilt designs using each block. Before long, I had a bunch of quilt designs all ready and waiting to be compiled into a book.

The Kaleidoscope block is one of my favorite blocks because it's fun to play with, and when multiple blocks are set side by side they form wonderful secondary designs. Plus, when combined with paper-piecing techniques, the blocks are easy to make. If you're new to paper piecing, and to quilting in general, you may want to start with "Shadow Play" (page 14) or "Mocha Latte" (page 22). If you're a more experienced quilter, you might pick one of the more complex designs, such as "Spinning My Blues Away" (page 66) or "Raspberry Truffle" (page 72). All of the projects in this book include step-by-step cutting and stitching instructions, as well as full-size patterns, to make constructing the quilts a breeze for any skill level. Don't shy away from a block with more pieces; it's not more difficult, it will just take longer to make.

Quilting is a wonderful creative outlet and a joy to share with everyone. I hope this book will ignite your individuality and inspire you to make these quilts your own.

In this section, you'll find valuable information for the successful completion of your quilt. All the special techniques needed to complete your quilt are covered on the following pages. Detailed instructions for specific quilting techniques, such as rotary cutting, machine piecing, machine quilting, and binding are not included because there are many excellent books available at your local quilt shop or library that cover these topics. I encourage you to make use of those resources for any additional information.

Fabric Selection

I love cotton fabrics and find that they provide the best results with the least amount of frustration. Besides, there are so many beautiful cotton fabrics available today—it's hard to resist them.

However, not all cotton fabrics are created equal. You've probably noticed that some cotton fabrics feel different from others, and some are easier to sew and press than others. There are several reasons for this, but the main reason is the choice of the base fabric, or greige (usually pronounced "gray") goods that are used. Most cotton fabrics are printed on bleached 100%-cotton muslin. This muslin is available in many different qualities and many different weaves (number of threads per inch in each direction). Other factors that can affect fabrics are the type of dyes used and the finishes that are added after the printing process.

In general, fabrics that have more threads per inch in each direction have a tighter weave. The tight weave is an advantage for paper piecing because the edges won't fray as much when handled and pieces cut on the bias hardly stretch at all. These fabrics have a smooth texture that makes them easier to press and they'll give you sharp, crisp points. Consequently, I recommend that whenever possible you choose fabrics with a tighter weave, such as batiks, to achieve the best results when constructing the quilts in this book.

Rotary Cutting

The projects in this book are all designed for rotary cutting and are easily pieced by machine. Use your cutter to cut borders as well as the patchwork strips and pieces in your project. All rotary-cutting measurements include ¼"-wide seam allowances. Basic rotary-cutting tools include a rotary cutter, an 18" x 24" cutting mat, a 6" x 24" acrylic ruler, and a 12½" square ruler for trimming blocks. You'll be able to make all the projects with these rulers, although I also find a 6" Bias Square® very useful for making cleanup cuts, crosscutting squares from strips, and squaring up smaller units.

Pressing

Pressing is one of the keys to precise piecing, and it's important to carefully press your work after stitching each seam. Pressing is planned so that the seam allowances will oppose one another when you sew the blocks and rows together. I like to press the seam allowances open to reduce bulk when joining paper-pieced units. Pressing directions are provided with each project.

When pressing paper-pieced units and blocks, use a hot, dry iron and always allow the pieces to cool before moving them from the pressing surface so that you don't distort them. Press the pieces on a lightly padded surface to prevent the seam allowances from creating a ridge on the right side of the unit. If you are pressing an area with multiple seams, place a pressing cloth over the piece to protect your fabrics from becoming glazed and shiny. To avoid shrinking the paper foundation and transferring ink onto your iron, always press on the fabric side of the units and blocks. Place a scrap of muslin under the pieces to avoid transferring ink to your pressing surface.

Paper Piecing

Paper piecing is a method of unit and block construction in which strips or precut pieces of fabric are sewn to a paper foundation in numerical order. Paper piecing requires a little more fabric than other piecing methods, but the greater accuracy you can achieve makes the extra fabric worthwhile.

Working with Grain Lines and Directional Fabrics

The paper to which you sew the fabric provides stability, so you don't need to worry too much about the grain of the fabric, except for those pieces that will be on the outside edges of the block. If possible, I do try to cut these pieces so that the edges are on the straight of grain. For this reason, I precut half-square triangles for units or blocks that have triangles in the outside corners.

I recommend using nondirectional printed or batik fabrics for the background of the units or blocks. Using a directional fabric can be distracting because the grain line and print will be going in different directions.

You can use a directional fabric, such as a stripe, to create a design element in some pieces of the unit or block. However, you'll need to precut those pieces so that the stripe is positioned consistently in each block.

Paper Foundations

You'll need one paper foundation pattern for each unit in each block. One way to make the paper foundations is to photocopy the designs. Be sure to check the accuracy of the copy against the original, and make all the

reproductions for each project on the same copy machine from the same original design; never copy another copy. For a nominal fee, most copy shops will remove the binding of this book and replace it with a spiral binding to make using it on a copy machine even easier.

The foundation paper you use should hold up during the sewing process and be easy to remove when the project is complete. You can use vellum, lightweight copy paper, or paper made specifically for foundations, such as Papers for Foundation Piecing, available from Martingale & Company. I prefer this type of paper because it reproduces the patterns accurately and tears away easily.

Test Your Foundation Paper

To check the suitability of your foundation paper, thread your sewing machine and adjust the stitch length as instructed in "Preparing to Sew" on page 7. Sew through a single sheet of paper. If the paper tears as you sew, it's too flimsy to use for foundation piecing. If you try to tear the paper away from the stitched line and it doesn't come away easily, the paper is too strong.

After you make the number of copies specified for your project, cut apart the units ½" from the outside sewing line. This makes the paper foundation easier to maneuver under the presser foot. And, if the fabric pieces extend beyond the paper foundation, you know the pieces are large enough to allow for the seam allowance around the outer edges.

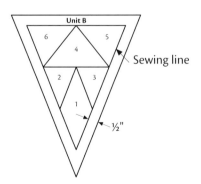

Color-Code the Patterns

You can color-code or mark your patterns so that you sew the correct fabric to the proper place in your units or blocks. I make an extra copy of the paper foundation, write the color or fabric description on each piece, and place it next to my sewing machine so I can easily see where the different fabrics go as I work.

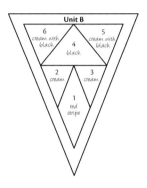

shaped piece, making sure to include at least a ¼" seam allowance on all sides of the template.

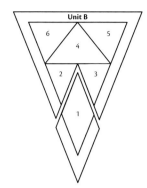

Precutting Pieces

Unlike traditional piecing, the fabric pieces used in paper piecing don't need to be cut the exact size of the areas they will cover. They just need to be large enough to fill the area on the pattern and also provide a generous seam allowance after the fabric is sewn and pressed. I simply cut strips of the desired fabric ½" to ¾" wider than the area that needs to be covered. For most of the projects, I sew the strips in place (following the numerical order) and then trim the excess strip, making sure to leave a generous seam allowance. I've found this method to be the most efficient use of the fabric strips. On the other hand, you may wish to precut the strips into squares or rectangles; however, this could require yardage adjustments that have not been provided.

When making a unit or block with odd-shaped pieces, or if I'm using a directional print, I make an extra copy of the block and then use a rotary cutter to cut out the piece on what would be the stitching lines. I then use the paper template to "rough cut" the odd-

Sorting Your Strips

When I have strips of the same fabric in similar widths for a project, I use a permanent marker to write the piece number in the selvage. That way I don't accidentally use a strip of the wrong width. When using batik fabrics, after I've decided which side I want to use for the "right" side, I use a permanent marker to label the strip on the selvage accordingly. In both instances, I begin using the strip at the unmarked end so that I don't lose my labels.

Preparing to Sew

Before you begin paper piecing, consider the following important points:

- Some patterns are the mirror image of the block you see in the diagrams. This is because the blocks are sewn from the marked side of the pattern, which is the reverse of the finished block. For symmetrical blocks the patterns and finished blocks look the same, but for asymmetrical blocks the finished blocks are mirror images of the patterns.

• Prepare your sewing machine with a size 90/14 needle and use an open-toe presser foot for good visibility. Then adjust your stitch length to a shorter-than-usual setting, 13 to 16 stitches per inch. This is approximately 1.8 on a sewing machine that has a stitch-length range of 0 to 5. The larger needle and smaller stitch length will allow you to remove the paper easily. However, don't make the stitches too short, because you'll have difficulty removing stitches if you sew a piece incorrectly.

• If you need to repair a torn piece of foundation paper, use removable tape. Be careful not to iron directly on the tape.

• Stitch on the printed side of the paper foundation and sew exactly on the line. Begin stitching every seam at least ¼" before the seam line and finish ¼" beyond the seam line.

• Press after sewing each fabric piece, or else you may get a tuck in the fabric and the pieces will not be the correct size. After sewing each piece, trim the seam allowance to ¼" before adding the next piece. (You'll find more instructions about trimming in the next section, "Basic Paper Piecing.")

Basic Paper Piecing

Before you begin, cut a piece of template plastic about 3" x 9". You can use lightweight cardboard if you don't have template plastic; however, template plastic is sturdier and will last longer. You'll use the plastic rectangle to fold the paper back on the foundation before trimming the fabric pieces. You'll also need a small ruler. I like to use a 2" x 8" ruler, but you can also use a 1" x 12" or an Add-a-Quarter ruler.

1. Turn the foundation so that the blank (unmarked) side of the paper is facing up. Position the fabric for piece 1, right side up, to cover area 1. Using the light from your sewing machine or another light source, look through the fabric and paper to make sure that area 1 is completely covered, with ample seam allowance around the entire area. Turn the paper and fabric over, being careful not to move the fabric, and pin the fabric in place through the marked side of the paper, using small-headed or flat-headed pins. Place the pin parallel to the seam line between areas 1 and 2.

2. Place a fabric strip for piece 2 on top of piece 1, right sides together. Make sure the fabric extends beyond the sewing line between areas 1 and 2 for the seam allowance.

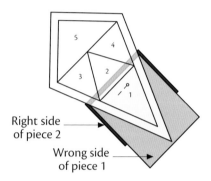

Right side of piece 2

Wrong side of piece 1

3. Holding the layers in place, carefully position the unit under your sewing machine's presser foot, paper side up. Sew directly on the line between areas 1 and 2, starting ¼" before the line and extending ¼" beyond.

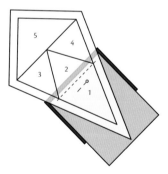

4. Clip the threads close to the paper on the front and back. Open piece 2 and remove the pin from piece 1. Hold the unit up to the light and look through the fabric to make sure the edges of piece 2 extend beyond the seam lines for area 2. Trim the excess part of the strips for pieces 1 and 2.

5. Refold the fabrics with right sides together, and then fold the paper back to reveal the seam allowance. Place a ruler along the edge of the paper and trim the seam allowance to a scant ¼". Open the fabrics so that both pieces are right side up and press the seam allowances to one side with a dry iron.

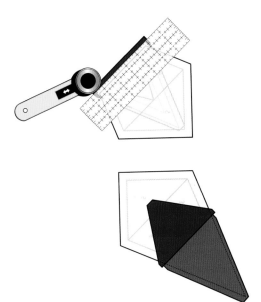

6. Place the plastic rectangle on the line between pieces 2 and 3, and fold the paper back along the plastic to expose the seam allowance. Place a ruler on the fold and trim the excess fabric so that it extends ¼" from the folded line. This trimming creates a straight edge upon which you can line up your next fabric piece, making placement much easier.

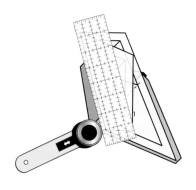

7. Align piece 3 with the newly cut edge of piece 2, right sides together. Holding the layers in place, carefully position the unit under your sewing machine's presser foot, paper side up. Sew directly on the line between areas 2 and 3 in the same manner as before. Open the fabrics so that both pieces are right side up; press the seam allowances to one side. Place the plastic rectangle on the line between pieces 2 and 4, and fold the paper back along the plastic to expose the seam allowance. Then place a ruler on the fold as shown and trim the excess fabric so that it extends ¼" from the folded line.

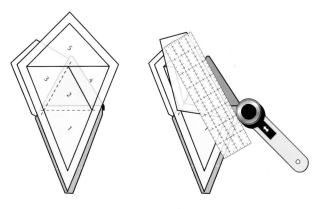

8. Continue in this manner, adding pieces in numerical order until the pattern is completely covered with fabric pieces.

9. Lay the unit, fabric side down (marked paper foundation up), on a cutting mat. Align a ruler's ¼" line with the outside sewing line, and then use a rotary cutter to trim the paper and fabrics ¼" from the sewing line on all sides.

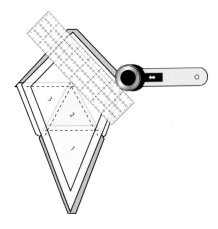

10. Do not remove the paper yet. Leave the paper foundation in place until the block is completed. Units are easier to align this way and won't become distorted by the tearing process. After sewing the units together into blocks, I remove the paper foundation from the center of the block and leave the paper around the outer edges. This makes sewing the blocks together easier. You can, however, wait and remove all the paper after the quilt top is completed.

Paper Removal

To remove the paper, gently tug against the stitching line, and the paper will pull away from the stitching. To remove the paper strips in the seam allowance, use a pair of tweezers. Don't fret too much about removing every tiny bit of paper.

Chain Piecing

Take the speed and accuracy of paper piecing to a new level by chain piecing the units just as you would in traditional patchwork. With chain piecing, you'll finish the multiple units required for the blocks in a fraction of the time. I recommend that before you begin chain piecing, you make one of each unit you'll need. That way you'll get a feel for how the unit goes together.

Referring to "Basic Paper Piecing," position a piece 1 and a piece 2 on the unmarked side of a foundation and sew the seam between the pieces. Immediately position another piece 1 and piece 2 on the next foundation and stitch the seam between those pieces. Don't stop between foundations to cut the threads.

After sewing enough units for one block, clip the threads between the units, press the seams, and trim the seam allowances to ¼". Then add piece 3 to the units in the same manner. Continue adding pieces in numerical order until the pattern is completely covered with fabric pieces.

Joining Units

For a perfect match every time, use a pin to help you match the seam intersections of your units. Place the two units right sides together and, working on the wrong side of the top unit, insert a pin into the corner of the stitching line at one end of the seam you're matching. Hold the pieces together as you insert the pin into the bottom unit, making sure the pin comes out at the corner point of the bottom unit. It may take a few tries, but by peeking underneath you'll hit the point exactly. In a similar manner, insert a pin at the other end of the unit and at each seam intersection in between.

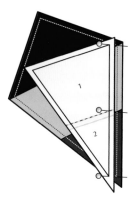

Pinch the two units together, matching the raw edges along the seam. Pin the pieces together securely. Remove the seam-matching pins and sew the seam.

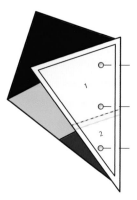

To ensure a good match at the seam intersections and to prevent the foundations from shifting during sewing, machine baste the seam intersections using a slightly larger-than-usual stitch and sewing a scant ¼" seam allowance. Open the seam and check that you have a good match. If you need to adjust the matching point, simply remove the basting stitches, adjust the pieces, and baste the seam again. Once you're satisfied with the seam, sew the seam line with a smaller stitch length.

Squaring Up Blocks

After stitching the units together to make the block, square up the block, keeping the design centered. To square up a block, line up the vertical and horizontal center lines of the block with the centerlines of the desired-size square on a square ruler. For example, the centerline of a 12½" square is the 6¼" line. Trim the first two sides of the block, and then turn the block around and trim the other two sides.

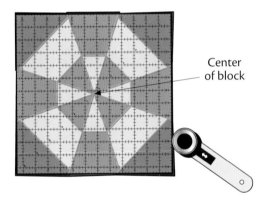

Center of block

Assembling the Quilt Top

1. Refer to the diagram for the particular quilt you are making to lay out the blocks and any other required pieces in the proper order. Sew the blocks together along the outer solid line on the foundation as indicated in the instructions, making sure to match the intersecting seams as needed.

2. After each seam is stitched and before it's pressed, remove the foundation paper from the stitched seam allowances *only*. To do this, gently tear the paper as if you were tearing perforated stamps. A gentle tug against the seam will give you a head start in loosening the paper from the stitching. Press the seam allowances as instructed for the project.

3. Refer to "Adding Borders" at right to add any borders to the quilt top. Remove the remaining paper foundations from the wrong side of the blocks. Gently press the completed quilt top.

Adding Borders

Borders can be simple strips of one or more fabrics. They can also be pieced or appliquéd and used in combination with plain strips. I've used a variety of border styles for the quilts in this book. Of course, you may choose to omit a border, but you will need to adjust yardages accordingly.

Prepare border strips a few inches longer than you will actually need; you'll trim them to the correct length once you know the final dimensions of your quilt top. To find the correct measurement for the border strips, always measure through the center of the quilt, not at the outside edges. This ensures that the borders are of equal length on opposite sides of the quilt and helps keep your quilt square.

Unless instructed otherwise, cut strips on the crosswise grain, selvage to selvage, and join them end to end with a diagonal seam to achieve the desired length. Press the seam allowances open so that they lie flat and are inconspicuous. Try to place the seams randomly around the quilt to make them less noticeable. I also prefer to attach the side borders first, and then add strips to the two remaining edges.

Borders with Butted Corners

Follow these instructions when adding borders with butted corners to your quilt.

1. Lay two strips across the center of the quilt top from top to bottom. Trim both ends even with the raw edges of the quilt.

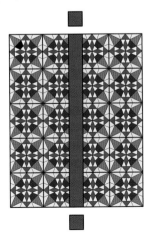

2. Mark the center of the border strips and the center of the sides of the quilt top. Pin the borders to the sides of the quilt top, matching centers and ends. Ease or slightly stretch the quilt top to fit the border strip as necessary. Sew the side borders in place with a ¼"-wide seam allowance and press the seam allowances toward the border strips.

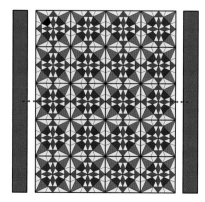

Mark centers.

3. Repeat the process for the top and bottom borders, measuring across the borders you just added.

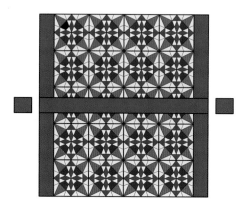

Pieced Borders

I love using pieced borders—they add a lot of interest to a quilt. However, they also require accurate seam allowances and careful pressing so that everything will fit together correctly. You'll notice in the instructions that when a plain border is sewn to the quilt center prior to the addition of a pieced border, the strips for the plain border need to be cut to specific lengths. The accuracy of the plain border is crucial in order for the pieced border to fit properly. Cut your plain borders to the specified lengths and ease them onto the quilt if necessary. I've indicated the correct measurement of the quilt center, including the plain border and seam allowances, so you can make sure your quilt is *mathematically* the right size.

Finishing Techniques

Once your quilt top is done, you're ready to move on to the finishing stages.

Backing and Batting

For the quilt backing, cut a piece of fabric 4" to 6" larger than the quilt top (2" to 3" on all sides). For quilts wider than the width of your fabric, you'll need to piece the backing. For most quilts in this book, I've listed enough backing fabric to piece the backing with one seam, leaving enough leftover fabric to cut a hanging sleeve, if desired. When piecing the backing, be sure to trim off the selvages before sewing the pieces together. Press the seam allowance open to reduce bulk.

Many types of batting are available today. The type you select will depend on whether you plan to hand or machine quilt your quilt. For machine quilting, a cotton batting works best, because it won't move or slip between the quilt top and backing. Whatever type of batting you choose, the piece should be large enough to allow an extra 2" around all edges of the quilt top.

If you plan to have your quilt professionally machine quilted, check with the long-arm quilter to see which type of batting is preferred and how you should prepare your backing.

Layering and Basting

All of the quilts in this book are machine quilted. If you plan to machine quilt your quilt using your home sewing machine, follow these instructions to sandwich your layers together.

Before you layer the quilt, give the quilt top and backing a careful pressing. Remove the batting from its package and let it relax for at least 24 hours, or place it in your dryer on a cool setting to eliminate wrinkles.

Next, spread the backing, wrong side up, on a flat, clean surface. Anchor the backing with pins or masking tape, taking care not to stretch the fabric out of shape. Center the batting over the backing, smoothing out any wrinkles. Center the pressed quilt top, right side up, over the batting, smoothing out any wrinkles and making sure the edges of the quilt top are parallel with the edges of the backing. Note that you should always smooth outward from the center and along straight lines to ensure that the blocks and borders remain straight.

Baste the layers with size 2 rustproof safety pins. Place the pins 3" to 4" apart, and try to avoid areas where you intend to quilt. Finish by machine basting about ⅛" from the edges of the quilt top.

Spray Basting

Instead of pin basting, try using a temporary spray adhesive. Be sure to follow the manufacturer's instructions for whichever product you use. I prefer Sulky KK 2000 because it's odorless, clear, and nontoxic. It also has a nice, tight spray pattern, which reduces overspray. I prepare the backing the same as I would for pin basting. I spray the backing, spread out the batting, and spray again. Then I spread out the quilt top, gently patting it all over to make sure the edges are parallel with the edges of the backing.

Quilting

As a general rule, no unquilted areas should exceed 4" x 4". In addition, check the package of the batting you're using for recommendations concerning the appropriate amount of quilting. The density of quilting should be similar throughout the entire quilt so that the quilt will remain square and not become distorted. For more information on machine quilting, refer to *Machine Quilting Made Easy!* by Maurine Noble (Martingale & Company, 1994).

Squaring Up Your Quilt

After you complete the quilting, you'll need to trim the excess backing and batting, as well as square up your quilt before sewing on the binding. Make sure all the basting threads or pins have been removed, but leave the basting stitches around the outer edges. Align a ruler with the seam line of the outer border and measure the width of the outer border in several places. Using the narrowest measurement, position a ruler along the seam line of the outer border, and trim the excess batting and backing from all four sides. Use a large, square ruler to square up each corner.

Binding

I like a relatively narrow binding. For most of the quilts in this book, I wanted the binding to "disappear" so that the focus would be drawn to the center of the quilt. Consequently, I used the same fabric for the binding as for the outer border. I like a double-fold binding made with strips cut 2" wide and sewn with a ¼" seam allowance. With the lightweight cotton battings I prefer, this combination of strip width and seam allowance is perfect for completely filling the binding with batting while still allowing the folded edge of the binding to just cover the stitching.

Shadow Play

Finished Quilt Size: 64½" x 77" • Finished Block Size: 12" x 12"

Pieced by Nancy Mahoney; machine quilted by Kelly Wise

Alternating light and dark blocks create an interplay of shadows that move across this lap-sized quilt to form circles, waves, and elongated Xs. A pieced diamond border (that's easier to piece than it looks!) adds a dramatic finish.

Materials

Yardages are based on 42"-wide fabrics.

2½ yards *total* of assorted dark prints for blocks

2½ yards *total* of assorted light prints for blocks

1½ yards of black print #1 for inner border, middle diamond border, and middle-border corners

1⅜ yards of black print #2 for middle diamond border and outer border

1 yard of purple print for blocks and binding

½ yard *each* of 2 different green prints (green #1 and green #2) for middle diamond border

½ yard of orangish-yellow print for blocks

4½ yards of fabric for backing

70" x 82" piece of batting

Foundation paper

Template plastic

Cutting

Cut all strips across the width of the fabric. To make the templates for diamond pieces C and D, trace the patterns on pages 20 and 21 onto template plastic and cut them out.

From the assorted dark prints, cut a *total* of:
- 20 strips, 4" x 42"

From the assorted light prints, cut a *total* of:
- 20 strips, 4" x 42"

From the orangish-yellow print, cut:
- 3 strips, 5" x 42"; crosscut into 20 squares, 5" x 5". Cut each square in half diagonally to yield 40 triangles.

From the purple print, cut:
- 3 strips, 5" x 42"; crosscut into 20 squares, 5" x 5". Cut each square in half diagonally to yield 40 triangles.
- 8 strips, 2" x 42"

From *each* of the 2 green prints, cut:
- 2 strips, 5" x 42"; cut 7 pieces using template C (14 total)
- 1 strip, 4¾" x 42; cut 6 pieces using template D (12 total)

From black print #1, cut:
- 3 strips, 5" x 42"; cut 16 pieces using template C
- 3 strips, 4¾" x 42"; cut 14 pieces using template D
- 6 strips, 2" x 42"
- 4 rectangles, 5½" x 5¾"

From black print #2, cut:
- 3 strips, 5" x 42"; cut 16 pieces using template C
- 3 strips, 4¾" x 42; cut 14 pieces using template D
- 7 strips, 2" x 42"

Making the Blocks

1. Make 80 copies *each* of the unit A and B foundation patterns on page 19.

2. Refer to "Paper Piecing" on page 6 to paper piece 10 sets of four matching A and B units as follows:

    Piece 1: dark strip

    Piece 2: light strip

    Piece 3: purple triangle (for A units only)

Unit A.
Make 10 sets of
4 matching units.

Unit B.
Make 10 sets of
4 matching units that
correspond to A units.

3. Paper piece 10 sets of four matching A and B units as follows:

    Piece 1: light strip

    Piece 2: dark strip

    Piece 3: orangish-yellow triangle (for A units only)

Unit A.
Make 10 sets of
4 matching units.

Unit B.
Make 10 sets of
4 matching units that
correspond to A units.

4. Using four matching A units and four matching B units, sew each A unit to a B unit as shown to make quarter units. Press the seam allowances open. Using a square ruler, trim any excess fabric along two sides as shown, making sure the center of each unit forms a 90° (right) angle. This little bit of trimming will make sewing the units together easier and help the block lie flat. Make 20 sets of four matching units.

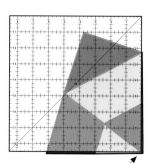

Trim excess fabric.

5. Arrange four matching quarter units as shown. Sew the units together in pairs and press the seam allowances open. Sew the pairs together, matching the seam intersections. Press the seam allowances open. Make 10 blocks with purple triangles and 10 blocks with orangish-yellow triangles.

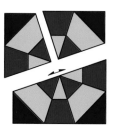 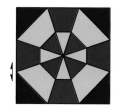

Make 10.

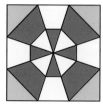

Make 10.

Making the Diamond Border

1. Using the C diamonds, sew a black #1 diamond and a black #2 diamond to opposite sides of each green #1 and #2 diamond as shown. Make 14 of these units.

Make 14.

2. Lay out four green #1 diamond units, three green #2 diamond units, one black #1 C diamond, and one black #2 C diamond as shown. Alternate the green #1 and green #2 diamonds, and place all of the black #1 diamonds on the opposite side from all of the black #2 diamonds. Sew the pieces together to make a side border strip. Press the seam allowances in one direction. Make two of these strips. Use a rotary cutter to trim the sides and ends of the border strips, making sure to leave ¼" beyond the points of the green diamonds for seam allowances. The border strips should measure 5½" x 63½".

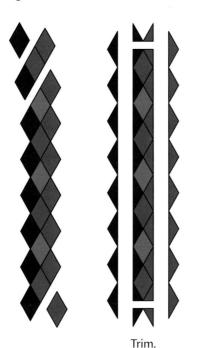

Trim.

3. Refer to step 1 to make 12 diamond units using the green #1, green #2, black #1, and black #2 D diamonds.

4. Repeat step 2, sewing three green #1 diamond units, three green #2 diamond units, one black #1 D diamond, and one black #2 D diamond together as shown in the assembly diagram on page 18 to make the top border. Make a second border strip for the bottom border. The border strips should measure 5¾" x 51½".

Assembling the Quilt Top

1. Lay out five rows of four blocks each, alternating the blocks with purple corners and the blocks with yellow corners as shown. When you are pleased with the arrangement, sew the blocks in each row together. Press the seam allowances in opposite directions from row to row. Sew the rows together and press the seam allowances in one direction. Your quilt top should measure 48½" x 60½".

2. Sew the 2"-wide black #1 strips together end to end. From the pieced strip, cut two 60½"-long strips, and sew them to the sides of the quilt top. Press the seam allowances toward the black border. From the remainder of the pieced strip, cut two 51½"-long

strips, and sew them to the top and bottom of the quilt; press. The quilt top should measure 51½" x 63½" for the diamond border to fit properly.

3. Sew the diamond side borders to opposite sides of the quilt top, making sure the black #1 diamonds are next to the inner border. Press the seam allowances toward the black inner border. Sew black #1 rectangles to the ends of the top and bottom diamond borders; press the seam allowances toward the rectangles. Sew the borders to the top and bottom of the quilt top and press the seam allowances toward the black inner border.

4. Sew the 2"-wide black #2 strips together end to end. Refer to "Adding Borders" on page 11 to measure the length of the quilt top and cut two strips to this length. Sew the strips to the sides of the quilt top. Press the seam allowances toward the outer border. Measure the width of the quilt top and cut two strips to this length from the remainder of the pieced strip. Sew these strips to the top and bottom of the quilt. Press the seam allowances toward the outer border.

Finishing

Cut and piece the backing fabric, and then layer the quilt top with batting and backing. After basting the layers together, hand or machine quilt as desired; see the quilting suggestion below. Trim the batting and backing so that the edges are even with the quilt top. Use the 2"-wide purple strips to make and attach the binding.

Quilting suggestion

Quilt assembly

18

Unit A

Unit B

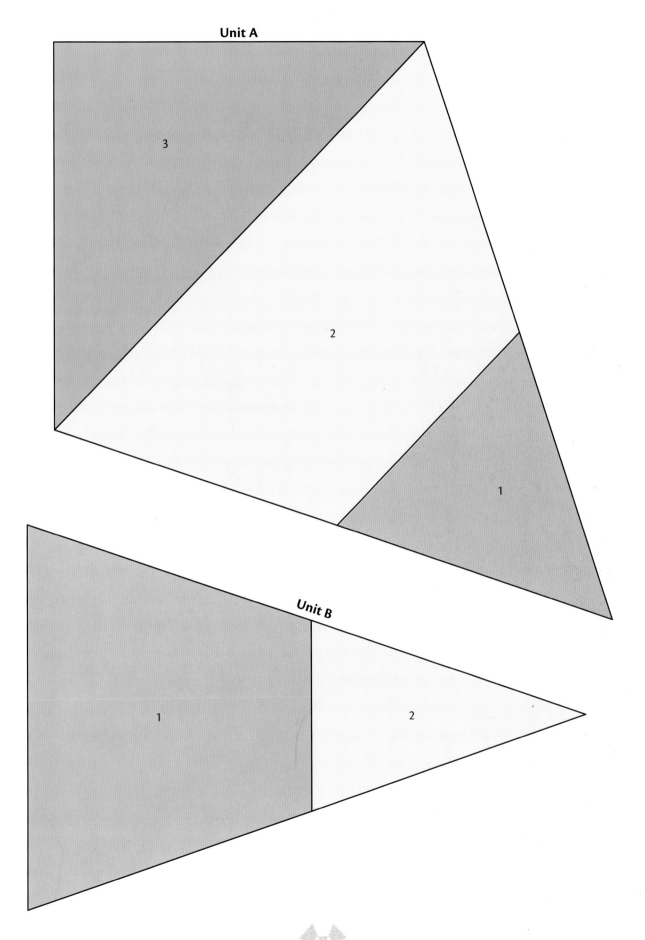

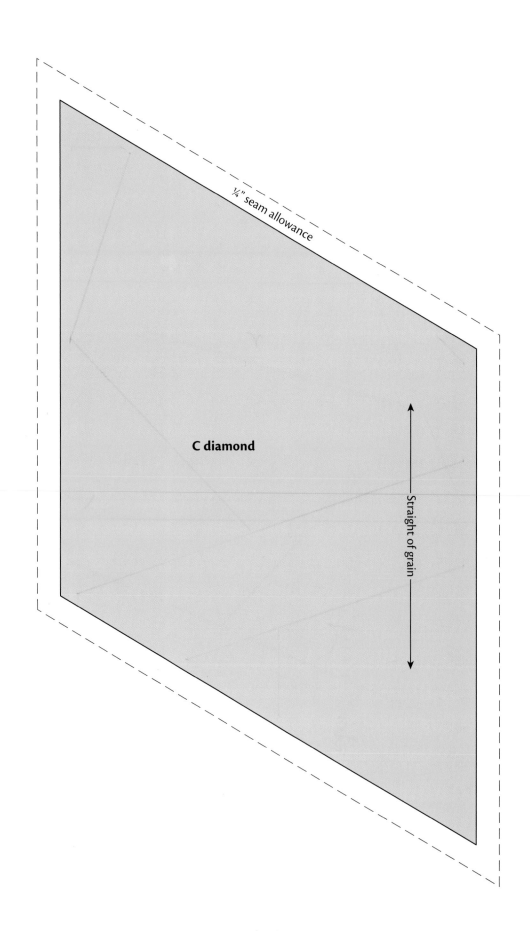

¼" seam allowance

C diamond

Straight of grain

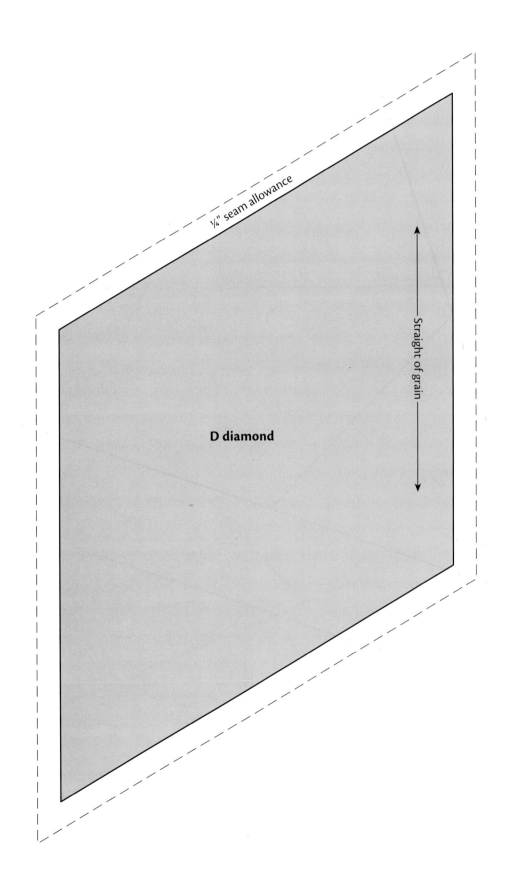

¼" seam allowance

Straight of grain

D diamond

Mocha Latte

Finished Quilt Size: 52½" x 65½" • Finished Block Size: 13" x 13"

Pieced by Dee Duckworth; machine quilted by Gloria Eckhart

A rich palette of chocolate-, coffee-, and cream-colored batiks mix with a shot of rust and green prints to create a delicious visual sensation. Add a couple of simple borders and you've got a treat guaranteed to warm you from head to toe.

Materials

Yardages are based on 42"-wide fabrics.

1⅝ yards of multicolored batik for inner border, outer border, and binding

⅞ yard of rust batik for blocks and middle border

⅔ yard of cream batik for blocks

⅝ yard of light-tan batik for blocks

½ yard of dark-brown batik for blocks

½ yard of brown-with-dots batik for blocks

½ yard of green-and-rust batik for blocks

½ yard of tan-and-green dots batik for blocks

¼ yard of tan-and-green floral batik for blocks

3½ yards of fabric for backing

58" x 71" piece of batting

Foundation paper

Cutting

Cut all strips across the width of the fabric.

From the rust batik, cut:
- 4 strips, 4½" x 42"
- 6 strips, 1½" x 42"

From the dark-brown batik, cut:
- 4 strips, 3½" x 42"

From the cream batik, cut:
- 6 strips, 3¼" x 42"

From the brown-with-dots batik, cut:
- 3 strips, 5" x 42"; crosscut into 24 squares, 5" x 5". Cut each square in half diagonally to yield 48 triangles.

From the green-and-rust batik, cut:
- 4 strips, 3½" x 42"

From the tan-and-green dots batik, cut:
- 4 strips, 3¼" x 42"

From the light-tan batik, cut:
- 4 strips, 4½" x 42"

From the tan-and-green floral batik, cut:
- 2 strips, 3¼" x 42"

From the multicolored batik, cut:
- 6 strips, 4½" x 42"
- 12 strips, 2" x 42"

Making the Blocks

1. Make 48 copies *each* of the unit A and B foundation patterns on pages 26 and 27.

2. Refer to "Paper Piecing" on page 6 to paper piece 48 A units as follows:

   Piece 1: rust strips, 4½" wide
   Piece 2: dark-brown strips
   Pieces 3 and 4: cream strips
   Piece 5: brown-with-dots triangles

Unit A.
Make 48.

3. Paper piece 34 B units as follows:
   Piece 1: green-and-rust strips
   Pieces 2 and 3: tan-and-green dots strips
   Piece 4: light-tan strips

Unit B.
Make 34.

4. Paper piece 14 B units as follows:
   Piece 1: green-and-rust strips
   Pieces 2 and 3: tan-and-green floral strips
   Piece 4: light-tan strips

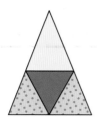

Unit B.
Make 14.

5. Sew each A unit to a B unit as shown to make a quarter unit. Make the number of units indicated of each combination. Press the seam allowances open. Using a square ruler, trim any excess fabric along two sides as shown, making sure the center of each unit forms a 90° (right) angle and leaving ¼" beyond all points on the units for seam allowances. This little bit of trimming will

make sewing the units together easier and help the block lie flat.

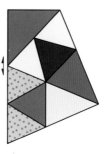 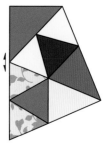

Make 34. Make 14.

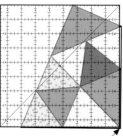

Trim excess fabric.

6. Arrange four quarter units as shown. Sew the units together in pairs and press the seam allowances open. Sew the pairs together, matching the seam intersections. Press the seam allowances open. Make four A blocks, six B blocks, and two C blocks.

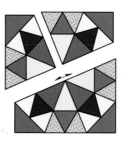 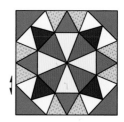

Block A.
Make 4.

Block B.
Make 6.

Block C.
Make 2.

Assembling the Quilt Top

1. Lay out four rows of three blocks each, positioning the blocks as shown. Sew the blocks in each row together. Press the seam allowances in opposite directions from row to row. Sew the rows together and press the seam allowances in one direction.

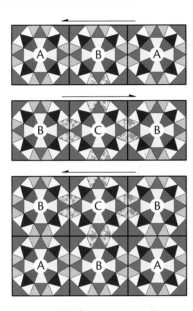

2. Sew the 2"-wide multicolored-batik strips together end to end. Refer to "Adding Borders" on page 11 to measure the length of the quilt top. From the pieced strip, cut two strips to this length and sew them to the sides of the quilt top. Press the seam allowances toward the border. Measure the width of the quilt top. From the remainder of the pieced strip, cut two strips to this length and sew them to the top and bottom of the quilt top to complete the inner border. Press the seam allowances toward the border. Set aside the remainder of the pieced strip for the binding.

3. In the same manner, sew the 1½"-wide rust strips together end to end, and then measure, cut, and sew the strips to the quilt top for the middle border. Lastly, join the 4½"-wide multicolored-batik strips end to end; measure, cut, and sew the strips to the

quilt top for the outer border. Press all seam allowances toward the just-added borders.

Quilt assembly

Finishing

Cut and piece the backing fabric, and then layer the quilt top with batting and backing. After basting the layers together, hand or machine quilt as desired; see the quilting suggestion below. Trim the batting and backing so that the edges are even with the quilt top. Use the remaining pieced strip of 2"-wide multicolored batik to make and attach the binding.

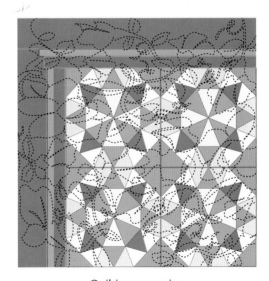

Quilting suggestion

Unit A

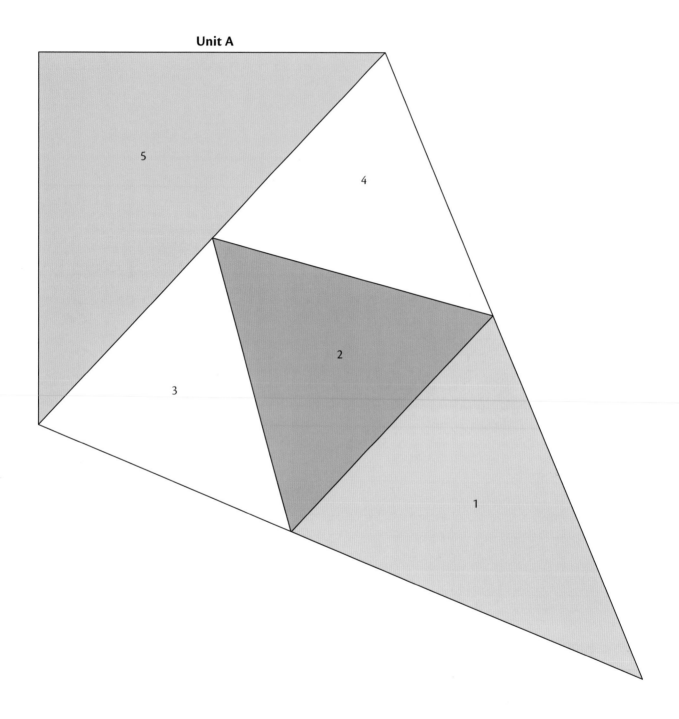

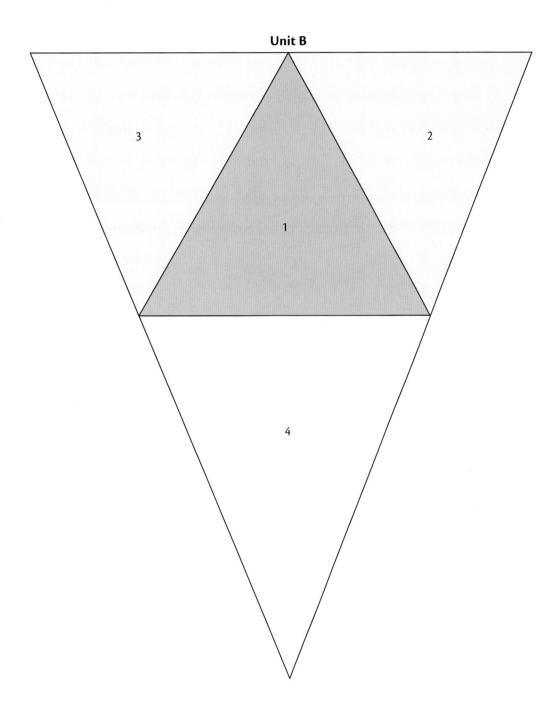

Unit B

Fractured Crystals

Finished Quilt Size: 52½" x 65½" • **Finished Block Size:** 13" x 13"

Pieced and machine quilted by Silvia Ciofalo

Complex crystal shapes come together as easy as pie with paper-piecing techniques. In no time at all, you'll have a flurry of perfect points!

Materials

Yardages are based on 42"-wide fabrics.

3⅛ yards of cream batik for blocks and middle border

¾ yard of dark-blue batik #1 for blocks

2⅛ yards of dark-blue batik #2 for blocks, inner border, outer border, and binding

1 yard of medium-blue batik for blocks

¾ yard of bright-blue batik for blocks

½ yard of light-blue batik for blocks

3⅜ yards of fabric for backing

58" x 71" piece of batting

Foundation paper

Cutting

Cut all strips across the width of the fabric.

From the bright-blue batik, cut:

- 4 strips, 3" x 42"
- 4 strips, 2½" x 42"

From the cream batik, cut:

- 15 strips, 1½" x 42"
- 8 strips, 2¾" x 42"
- 14 strips, 1¾" x 42"
- 16 strips, 2" x 42"

From the medium-blue batik, cut:

- 10 strips, 2¾" x 42"

From the dark-blue batik #1, cut:

- 14 strips, 2" x 42"

From the dark-blue batik #2, cut:

- 18 strips, 2" x 42"
- 6 strips, 4½" x 42"

From the light-blue batik, cut:

- 7 strips, 2" x 42"

Making the Blocks

Before you begin, set aside twelve 2"-wide dark blue #2 strips for the inner border and binding and six cream 1½"-wide strips for the middle border.

1. Make 48 copies *each* of the unit A and B foundation patterns on pages 32 and 33.

2. Refer to "Paper Piecing" on page 6 to paper piece 48 A units as follows:

   Piece 1: bright-blue strips, 3" wide
   Piece 2: cream strips, 1½" wide
   Piece 3: cream strips, 2¾" wide
   Piece 4: medium-blue strips
   Piece 5: cream strips, 1¾" wide
   Piece 6: dark-blue #1 strips
   Pieces 7 and 8: cream strips, 2" wide
   Piece 9: dark-blue #2 strips, 2" wide

Unit A.
Make 48.

3. Paper piece 34 B units as follows:

Piece 1: dark-blue #1 strips
Pieces 2 and 3: cream strips, 2" wide
Piece 4: light-blue strips
Piece 5: cream strips, 1¾" wide
Piece 6: medium-blue strips
Piece 7: cream strips, 2¾" wide
Piece 8: bright-blue strips, 2½" wide
Piece 9: cream strips, 1½" wide

Unit B.
Make 34.

4. Paper piece 14 B units as follows:

Piece 1: dark-blue #1 strips
Pieces 2 and 3: cream strips, 2" wide
Piece 4: dark-blue #2 strips, 2" wide
Piece 5: cream strips, 1¾" wide
Piece 6: medium-blue strips
Piece 7: cream strips, 2¾" wide
Piece 8: bright-blue strips, 2½" wide
Piece 9: cream strips, 1½" wide

Unit B.
Make 14.

5. Sew each A unit to a B unit as shown to make quarter units. Make the number of units indicated of each combination. Press the seam allowances open. Using a square ruler, trim any excess fabric along two sides as shown, making sure the center of each unit forms a 90° (right) angle and leaving ¼" beyond all points on the units for seam

allowances. This little bit of trimming will make sewing the units together easier and help the blocks lie flat.

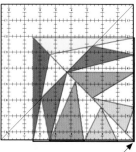

Make 34.   Make 14.

Trim excess fabric.

6. Arrange four quarter units from step 5 as shown. Sew the units together in pairs and press the seam allowances open. Sew the pairs together, matching the seam intersections. Press the seam allowances open. Make the number of blocks indicated.

Block A.
Make 4.

Block B.
Make 6.

Block C.
Make 2.

30

Assembling the Quilt Top

1. Lay out four rows of three blocks each, positioning the blocks as shown. Sew the blocks together in each row. Press the seam allowances in opposite directions from row to row. Sew the rows together and press the seam allowances in one direction.

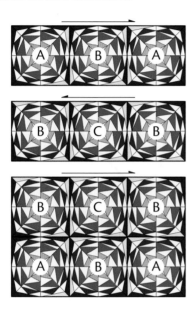

2. Sew the remaining 2"-wide dark-blue #2 strips together end to end. Refer to "Adding Borders" on page 11 to measure the length of the quilt top. From the pieced strip, cut two strips to this length and sew them to the sides of the quilt top. Press the seam allowances toward the border. Measure the width of the quilt top. From the remainder of the pieced strip, cut two strips to this length and sew them to the top and bottom of the quilt top to complete the inner border. Press the seam allowances toward the border. Set aside the remainder of the dark-blue pieced strip for the binding.

3. In the same manner, sew the remaining 1½"-wide cream strips together end to end and then measure, cut, and sew the strips to the quilt top for the middle border. Lastly, join the 4½"-wide dark-blue #2 strips end to end; measure, cut, and sew them to the

quilt top for the outer border. Press all seam allowances toward the just-added borders.

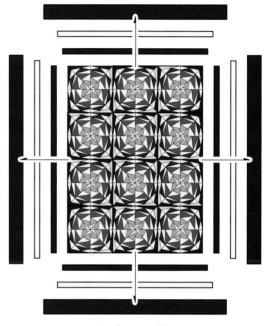

Quilt assembly

Finishing

Cut and piece the backing fabric, and then layer the quilt top with batting and backing. After basting the layers together, hand or machine quilt as desired; see the quilting suggestion below. Trim the batting and backing so that the edges are even with the quilt top. Use the remaining pieced strip of 2"-wide dark-blue #2 to make and attach the binding.

Quilting suggestion

Unit A

Unit B

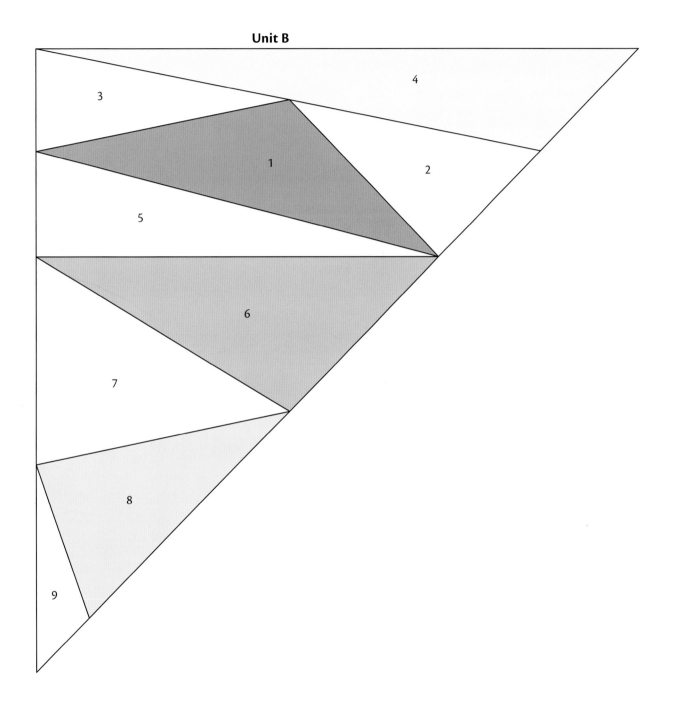

Dutch Treat

Finished Quilt Size: 62½" x 62½" • Finished Block Size: 12" x 12"

Pieced and machine quilted by Nancy Mahoney

When you think of Holland, windmills and tulips probably come to mind. In this quilt, you can combine the two, creating blades in tulip-bright colors that generate silent energy, just like the ones that dot the Dutch landscape.

Materials

Yardages are based on 42"-wide fabrics.

3½ yards of royal-blue batik for blocks, sashing, inner border, outer border, and binding

1⅛ yards of yellow batik for blocks

¼ yard of orange batik #1 for blocks

½ yard of orange batik #2 for blocks and middle border

½ yard of orange batik #3 for blocks

¾ yard of orange batik #4 for blocks

⅓ yard of blue batik #1 for blocks

⅜ yard of blue batik #2 for blocks

½ yard of blue batik #3 for blocks

¼ yard of teal batik for blocks

3¾ yards of fabric for backing

68" x 68" piece of batting

Foundation paper

Cutting

Cut all strips across the width of the fabric.

From the teal batik, cut:
- 3 strips, 2¼" x 42"

From the orange batik #1, cut:
- 3 strips, 2" x 42"

From the blue batik #1, cut:
- 4 strips, 2" x 42"

From the orange batik #2, cut:
- 4 strips, 2" x 42"
- 6 strips, 1" x 42"

From the blue batik #2, cut:
- 5 strips, 2" x 42"

From the orange batik #3, cut:
- 6 strips, 2" x 42"

From the blue batik #3, cut:
- 7 strips, 2" x 42"

From the orange batik #4, cut:
- 11 strips, 2" x 42"

From the yellow batik, cut:
- 5 strips, 7" x 42"

From the royal-blue batik, cut:
- 5 strips, 5¼" x 42"; crosscut into 32 squares, 5¼" x 5¼". Cut each square in half diagonally to yield 64 triangles.
- 8 strips, 2½" x 42"
- 14 strips, 1½" x 42"; crosscut *4 of the strips* into 12 strips, 1½" x 12½"
- 6 strips, 4½" x 42"
- 7 strips, 2" x 42"

Making the Blocks

1. Make 64 copies *each* of the unit A and B foundation patterns on pages 38 and 39.

2. Refer to "Paper Piecing" on page 6 to paper piece 64 A units as follows:

   Piece 1: teal strips

   Piece 2: orange #1 strips

   Piece 3: blue #1 strips

   Piece 4: orange #2 strips, 2" wide

   Piece 5: blue #2 strips

   Piece 6: orange #3 strips

   Piece 7: blue #3 strips

   Piece 8: orange #4 strips

   Piece 9: royal-blue triangles

Unit A.
Make 64.

3. Paper piece 64 B units as follows:

   Piece 1: yellow strips

   Pieces 2 and 3: royal-blue strips, 2½" wide

Unit B.
Make 64.

4. Sew each A unit to a B unit as shown to make quarter units. Make 64 units. Press the seam allowances open. Using a square ruler, trim any excess fabric along two sides as shown, making sure the center of each unit forms a 90° (right) angle and leaving ¼" beyond all points on the units for seam allowances. This little bit of trimming will make sewing the units together easier and help the blocks lie flat.

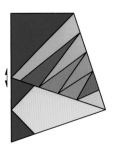

Make 64.

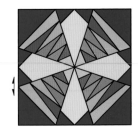

Trim excess fabric.

5. Arrange four quarter units from step 4 as shown. Sew the units together in pairs and press the seam allowances open. Sew the pairs together, matching the seam intersections. Press the seam allowances open. Make 16 blocks.

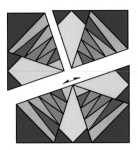

Make 16.

Assembling the Quilt Top

1. Lay out four blocks and three 1½" x 12½" royal-blue sashing strips as shown. Sew the pieces together to make a block row, pressing the seam allowances toward the sashing strips. Make four block rows total. The block rows should be 51½" long.

Make 4.

2. Sew four 1½"-wide royal-blue strips together end to end. From the pieced strip, cut three 51½"-long sashing strips. Sew the block rows and long sashing strips together as shown. Press the seam allowances toward the sashing strips.

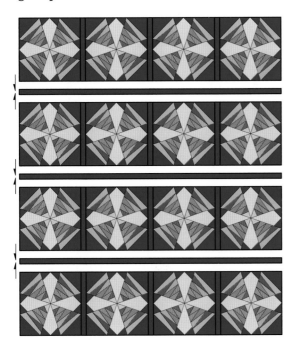

3. Sew the remaining 1½"-wide royal-blue strips together end to end. Refer to "Adding Borders" on page 11 to measure the length of the quilt top. From the pieced strip, cut two strips to this length and sew them to the sides of the quilt top. Press the seam allowances toward the royal-blue border. Measure the width of the quilt top. From the remainder of the pieced strip, cut two strips to this length and sew them to the top and bottom of the quilt top to complete the inner border. Press the seam allowances toward the border.

4. In the same manner, sew the 1"-wide orange #2 strips together end to end and then measure, cut, and sew the strips to the quilt top for the middle border. Lastly, join the 4½"-wide royal-blue strips end to end; measure, cut, and sew them to the quilt top for the

outer border. Press all seam allowances toward the just-added borders.

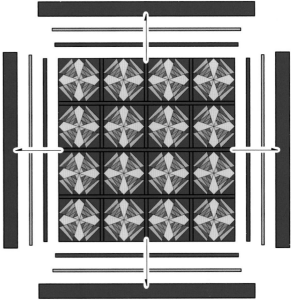

Quilt assembly

Finishing

Cut and piece the backing fabric, and then layer the quilt top with batting and backing. After basting the layers together, hand or machine quilt as desired; see the quilting suggestion below. Trim the batting and backing so that the edges are even with the quilt top. Use the 2"-wide royal-blue strips to make and attach the binding.

Quilting suggestion

Unit A

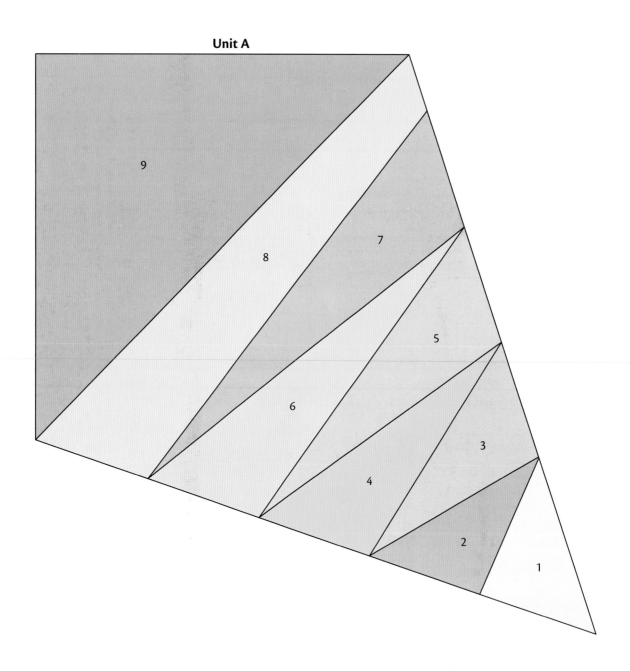

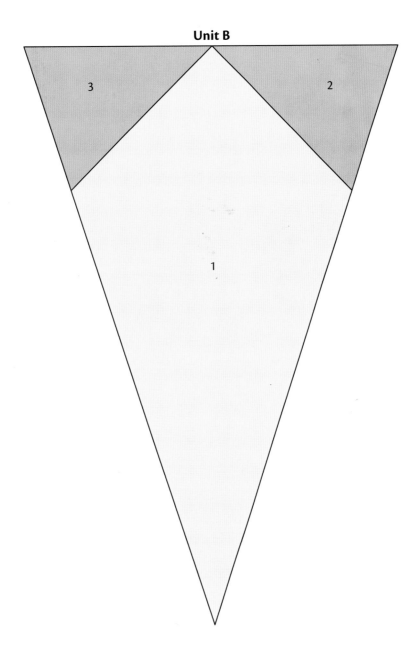

Unit B

3

2

1

Emeralds and Amethysts

Finished Quilt Size: 64½" x 64½" • **Finished Block Size:** 12" x 12"

Pieced and machine quilted by Elizabeth Allocco

Sparkling like the treasures in a jeweler's display case, these green-and-purple blocks create a stunning show against a black backdrop. Dig into your stash for an assortment of fabrics to make each block different and you're guaranteed to create your own precious gem.

Materials

Yardages are based on 42"-wide fabrics.

4⅜ yards of cream batik for blocks and pieced border

3⅓ yards *total* of assorted purple batiks for blocks and pieced middle border

2⅝ yards of black batik for blocks, sashing, borders, and binding

2⅛ yards *total* of assorted green batiks for blocks and pieced middle border

⅝ yard of bright-purple batik for blocks

4 yards of fabric for backing

70" x 70" piece of batting

Foundation paper

Cutting

Cut all strips across the width of the fabric. You may want to cut a few strips in each width, and then cut more strips as you need them. Depending on how efficiently you use the strips, you may not need all the strips listed. For this quilt, I recommend precutting some of the pieces as described on page 7.

From the assorted purple batiks, cut a *total* of:

- 11 strips, 2¼" x 42"
- 9 strips, 3¼" x 42"
- 11 strips, 5" x 42"

From the cream batik, cut:

- 21 strips, 2¼" x 42"
- 12 strips, 2" x 42"
- 13 strips, 1¾" x 42"
- 10 strips, 1½" x 42"
- 4 strips, 7" x 42"; crosscut into 48 rectangles, 3" x 7"
- 8 squares, 3" x 3"; cut each square in half diagonally to yield 16 triangles

From the bright-purple batik, cut:

- 4 strips, 4½" x 42"; crosscut into 32 squares, 4½" x 4½". Cut each square in half diagonally to yield 64 triangles.

From the assorted green batiks, cut a *total* of:

- 8 strips, 4" x 42"
- 6 strips, 2¼" x 42"
- 4 strips, 2½" x 42"
- 4 squares, 3" x 3"

From the black batik, cut:

- 13 strips, 1½" x 42"
- 14 strips, 1¼" x 42"; crosscut *4 of the strips* into 12 strips, 1¼" x 12½"
- 11 strips, 1⅜" x 42"
- 7 strips, 1⅝" x 42"
- 7 strips, 2" x 42"
- 8 squares, 3¾" x 3¾"; cut each square in half diagonally to yield 16 triangles

Making the Blocks

1. Make 64 copies *each* of the unit A and B foundation patterns on page 45.

2. Refer to "Paper Piecing" on page 6 to paper piece 64 A units as follows:

    Piece 1: assorted purple strips, 2¼" wide

    Pieces 2, 3, and 4: cream strips, 2" wide (or use precut pieces)

    Piece 5: assorted purple strips, 2¼" wide

    Pieces 6 and 7: cream strips, 2¼" wide (or use precut pieces)

    Piece 8: assorted purple strips, 3¼" wide

    Pieces 9 and 10: cream strips, 2¼" wide (or use precut pieces)

    Piece 11: black strips, 1½" wide

    Piece 12: bright-purple triangles

Unit A.
Make 64.

3. Paper piece 64 B units as follows:

    Piece 1: assorted green strips, 4" wide

    Pieces 2 and 3: cream strips, 1¾" wide (or use precut pieces)

    Piece 4: assorted green strips, 2¼" wide

    Pieces 5 and 6: cream strips, 1½" wide (or use precut pieces)

    Piece 7: assorted green strips, 2½" wide

Unit B.
Make 64.

4. Sew each A unit to a B unit as shown to make quarter units. Make 64 units. Press the seam allowances open. Using a square ruler, trim any excess fabric along two sides as shown, making sure the center of each unit forms a 90° (right) angle and leaving ¼" beyond all points on the units for seam allowances. This little bit of trimming will make sewing the units together easier and help the blocks lie flat.

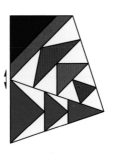

Make 64.   Trim excess fabric.

5. Arrange four quarter units from step 4 as shown. Sew the units together in pairs and press the seam allowances open. Sew the pairs together, matching the seam intersections. Press the seam allowances open. Make 16 blocks.

Make 16.

Making the Flying-Geese Border

1. Make 24 copies of the unit C foundation pattern on page 46 and four copies of the unit D foundation pattern on page 47.

2. With right sides facing up, cut 24 cream rectangles in half diagonally from top left to bottom right to make 48 half rectangles. Cut the remaining cream rectangles in half diagonally from bottom left to top right to make 48 reverse half rectangles.

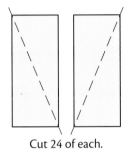

Cut 24 of each.

3. Refer to "Paper Piecing" to paper piece 24 C units as follows:

   Piece 1: assorted purple strips, 5" wide
   Piece 2: cream half rectangles
   Piece 3: cream reverse half rectangles
   Piece 4: assorted purple strips, 5" wide
   Piece 5: cream half rectangles
   Piece 6: cream reverse half rectangles

Unit C.
Make 24.

4. Paper piece four D units as follows:

   Piece 1: assorted green squares
   Pieces 2–5: cream triangles
   Pieces 6–9: black triangles

Unit D.
Make 4.

5. Sew six C units together as shown to make a border strip, making sure to rotate three units so that the points meet in the center of the strip. Press the seam allowances open. The border strip should measure 52¼" long. Repeat to make a total of four strips. Sew the 1⅜"-wide black strips together end to end. From this pieced strip, cut eight 52¼"-long sashing strips. Sew a black strip to each long side of the pieced border strips as shown. Press the seam allowances toward the black strips.

Make 4.

Assembling the Quilt Top

1. Lay out four blocks and three 1¼" x 12½" black sashing strips as shown. Sew the pieces together to make a block row, pressing the seam allowances toward the sashing strips. Make a total of four block rows. The block rows should be 50¾" long.

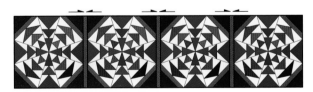

Make 4.

2. Sew four 1¼"-wide black strips together end to end. From the pieced strip, cut three 50¾"-long sashing strips. Sew the block rows and long sashing strips together as shown. Press the seam allowances toward the sashing strips.

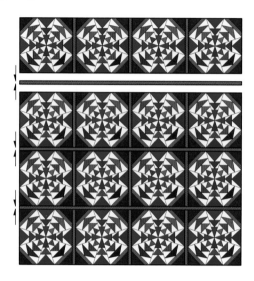

3. Sew the remaining 1¼"-wide black strips together end to end. From the pieced strip, cut two 50¾"-long strips and sew them to the sides of the quilt top. Press the seam allowances toward the black border. From the remainder of the pieced strip, cut two 52¼"-long strips and sew them to the top and bottom of the quilt top to complete the inner border. Press the seam allowances toward the black border.

4. Sew two flying-geese borders to opposite sides of the quilt top and press the seam allowances toward the flying-geese border. Sew a unit D block to each end of the remaining two flying-geese borders and press the seam allowances toward the pieced borders. Sew the borders to the top and bottom of the quilt top and press the seam allowances toward the flying-geese borders.

5. Sew the 1⅝"-wide black strips together end to end. Refer to "Adding Borders" on page 11 to measure the length of the quilt top and cut two strips to this length. Sew the strips to the sides of the quilt top. Press the seam allowances toward the outer border. Measure the width of the quilt top and cut two strips to this length from the remainder

of the pieced strip. Sew these strips to the top and bottom of the quilt. Press the seam allowances toward the outer border.

Quilt assembly

Finishing

Cut and piece the backing fabric, and then layer the quilt top with batting and backing. After basting the layers together, hand or machine quilt as desired; see the quilting suggestion below. Trim the batting and backing so that the edges are even with the quilt top. Use the 2"-wide black strips to make and attach the binding.

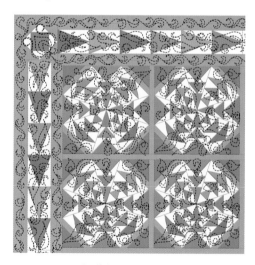

Quilting suggestion

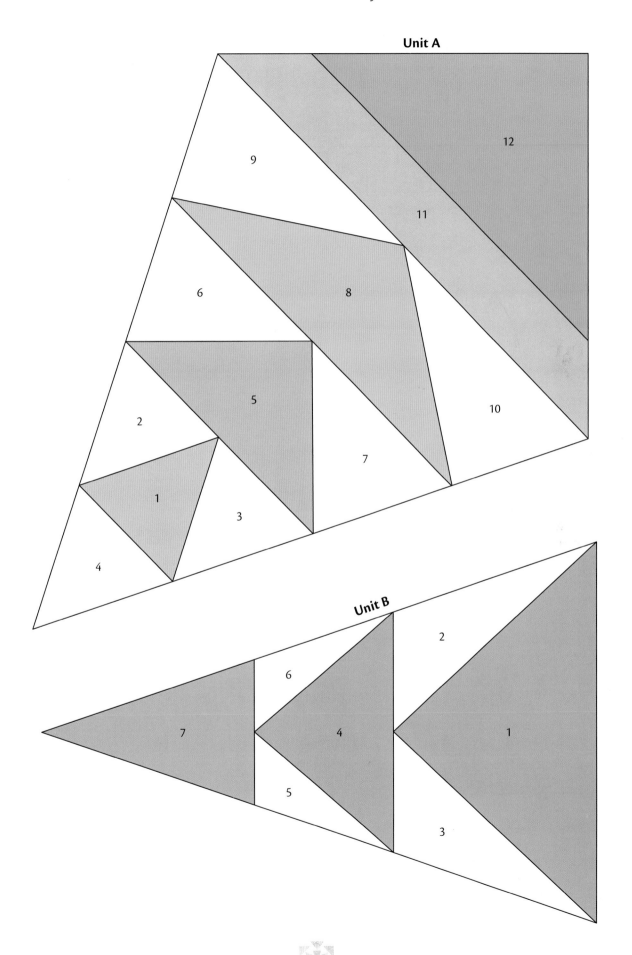

Unit C

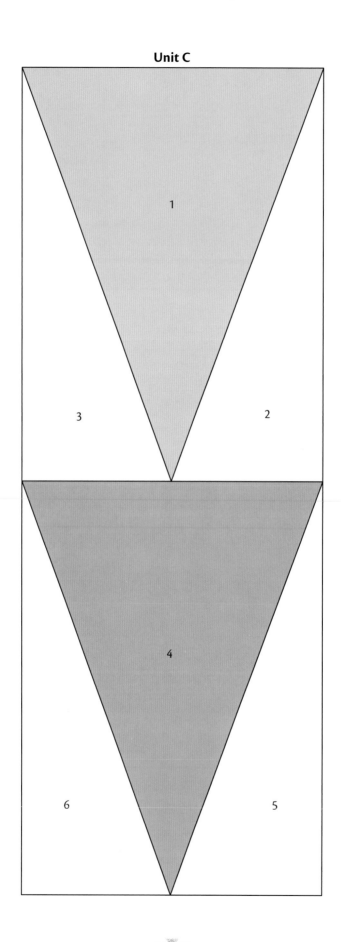

Unit D

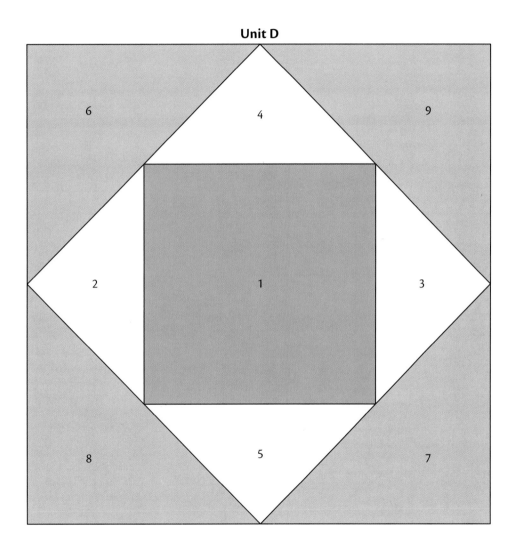

Star Rosettes

Finished Quilt Size: 58½" x 70½" • Finished Block Size: 12" x 12"

Pieced and machine quilted by Nancy Mahoney

You can't go wrong with a Star block, traditional or otherwise. Here, a combination of red, white, and black fabrics and a simple setting create a stellar design.

Materials

Yardages are based on 42"-wide fabrics.

3½ yards of black-on-white print for blocks

2 yards of black floral print for border and binding

1¼ yards of red-on-white print for blocks

1⅛ yards of red floral print for blocks

1 yard of black print for blocks

⅞ yard of red striped fabric for blocks

⅔ yard of red checked fabric for blocks

3⅝ yards of fabric for backing

64" x 76" piece of batting

Foundation paper

Cutting

Cut all strips across the width of the fabric unless otherwise indicated. You may want to cut a few strips in each width, and then cut more strips as you need them. Depending on how efficiently you use the strips, you may not need all the strips listed. For this quilt, you may find it helpful to precut some of the pieces as described on page 7.

From the red floral print, cut:
- 6 strips, 5½" x 42"

From the black-on-white print, cut:
- 16 strips, 3" x 42"
- 26 strips, 2½" x 42"

From the black print, cut:
- 10 strips, 2¾" x 42"

From the red-on-white print, cut:
- 4 strips, 3" x 42"
- 10 strips, 2½" x 42"

From the red striped fabric, cut:
- 5 strips, 5" x 42"

From the red checked fabric, cut:
- 7 strips, 2¾" x 42"

From the *lengthwise grain* of the black floral print, cut:
- 4 strips, 5½" x 62"
- 5 strips, 2" x 62"

Making the Blocks

1. Make 80 copies *each* of the unit A and B foundation patterns on pages 52 and 53.

2. Refer to "Paper Piecing" on page 6 to paper piece 80 A units as follows:

    Piece 1: red floral strips (or use precut pieces)

    Pieces 2 and 3: black-on-white strips, 2½" wide (or use precut pieces)

    Piece 4: black print strips

    Piece 5: red-on-white strips, 3" wide

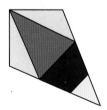

Unit A.
Make 80.

3. Paper piece 80 B units as follows:

Piece 1: red striped strips (or use precut pieces)

Pieces 2 and 3: red-on-white strips, 2½" wide (or use precut pieces)

Piece 4: red checked strips

Pieces 5 and 6: black-on-white strips, 3" wide (or use precut pieces)

Unit B.
Make 80.

4. Sew each A unit to a B unit as shown to make quarter units. Make 80 units. Press the seam allowances open. Using a square ruler, trim any excess fabric along two sides as shown, making sure the center of each unit forms a 90° (right) angle and leaving ¼" beyond all points on the unit for seam allowances. This little bit of trimming will make sewing the units together easier and help the blocks lie flat.

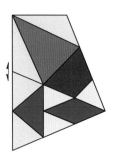
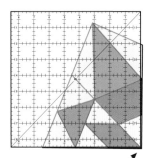

Trim excess fabric.

5. Arrange four quarter units from step 4 as shown. Sew the units together in pairs and press the seam allowances open. Sew the pairs together, matching the seam intersections. Press the seam allowances open. Make 20 blocks.

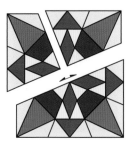
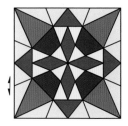

Make 20.

Assembling the Quilt Top

1. Lay out five rows of four blocks each as shown. Sew the blocks together in each row, pressing the seam allowances in opposite directions from row to row. Sew the rows together and press the seam allowances in one direction.

2. Refer to "Adding Borders" on page 11 to measure the length of the quilt top. Trim two 5½"-wide black floral strips to this length and sew them to the sides of the quilt top. Press the seam allowances toward the black border. Measure the width of the quilt top. Trim two black floral strips to this length and sew them to the top and bottom of the quilt for the border. Press the seam allowances toward the border.

Finishing

Cut and piece the backing fabric, and then layer the quilt top with batting and backing. After basting the layers together, hand or machine quilt as desired; see the quilting suggestion below. Trim the batting and backing so that the edges are even with the quilt top. Use the 2"-wide black floral strips to make and attach the binding.

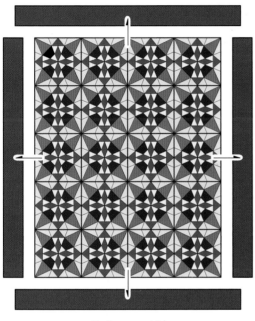

Quilt assembly

Quilting suggestion

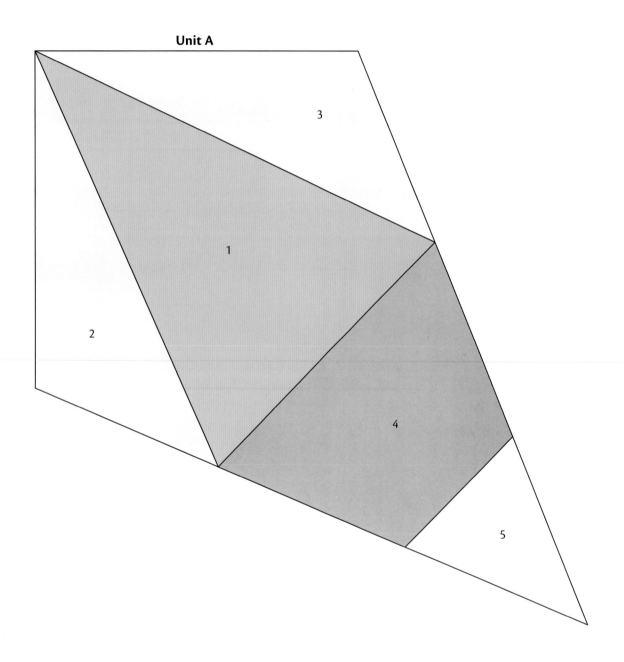

Unit A

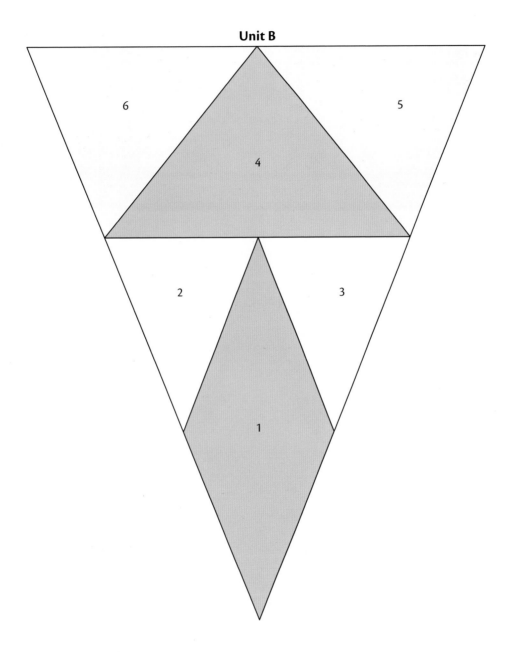

Unit B

Pinwheels in the Wind

Finished Quilt Size: 66½" x 66½" • **Finished Block Size:** 12" x 12"

Pieced and machine quilted by Gillian Smith

Memories of childhood toys are sure to spin through your mind with this colorful quilt. These pinwheels might not move when you blow on them, but they'll provide just as much fun as you breeze through the piecing.

Materials

Yardages are based on 42"-wide fabrics.

3⅜ yards of dark-purple batik for blocks, sashing, first and fourth borders, and binding

1⅜ yards of lavender batik for blocks and second border

1¼ yards of multicolored batik for blocks

1¼ yards of cream batik for blocks

1 yard of gold batik for blocks and third border

1 yard of rust batik for blocks

1 yard of gray-and-purple batik for blocks

⅝ yard of yellow batik for blocks

4¼ yards of fabric for backing

72" x 72" piece of batting

Foundation paper

Cutting

Cut all strips across the width of the fabric.

From the gray-and-purple batik, cut:

- 7 strips, 4" x 42"

From the yellow batik, cut:

- 8 strips, 2" x 42"

From the cream batik, cut

- 6 strips, 3½" x 42"
- 8 strips, 2" x 42"

From the rust batik, cut:

- 14 strips, 2" x 42"

From the lavender batik, cut:

- 16 strips, 2" x 42"
- 6 strips, 1¾" x 42"

From the dark-purple batik, cut:

- 16 strips, 2½" x 42"
- 8 strips, 1½" x 42"; crosscut *4 of the strips into 12 sashing strips, 1½" x 12½"*
- 6 strips, 1¼" x 42"
- 7 strips, 5" x 42"
- 7 strips, 2" x 42"

From the gold batik, cut:

- 6 strips, 3½" x 42"
- 6 strips, 1½" x 42"

From the multicolored batik, cut:

- 13 strips, 3" x 42"

Making the Blocks

1. Make 64 copies *each* of the unit A and B foundation patterns on pages 58 and 59.

2. Refer to "Paper Piecing" on page 6 to paper piece 64 A units as follows:

   Piece 1: gray-and-purple strips
   Piece 2: yellow strips
   Piece 3: cream strips, 3½" wide
   Piece 4: rust strips
   Piece 5: lavender strips, 2" wide
   Piece 6: dark-purple strips, 2½" wide

Unit A.
Make 64.

3. Paper piece 64 B units as follows:

   Piece 1: dark-purple strips, 2½" wide
   Piece 2: lavender strips, 2" wide
   Piece 3: rust strips
   Piece 4: cream strips, 2" wide
   Piece 5: gold strips, 3½" wide
   Piece 6: multicolored strips

Unit B.
Make 64.

4. Sew each A unit to a B unit as shown to make quarter units. Make 64 units. Press the seam allowances open. Using a square ruler, trim any excess fabric along two sides as shown, making sure the center of each

unit forms a 90° (right) angle and leaving ¼" beyond all points on the units for seam allowances. This little bit of trimming will make sewing the units together easier and help the blocks lie flat.

Make 64. Trim excess fabric.

5. Arrange four quarter units from step 4 as shown. Sew the units together in pairs and press the seam allowances open. Sew the pairs together, matching the seam intersections. Press the seam allowances open. Make 16 blocks.

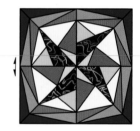

Make 16.

Assembling the Quilt Top

1. Lay out four blocks and three 1½" x 12½" dark-purple sashing strips as shown. Sew the pieces together to make a block row, pressing the seam allowances toward the sashing strips. Make a total of four block rows. The block rows should measure 51½" long.

Make 4.

2. Sew the remaining four 1½"-wide dark-purple strips together end to end. From the pieced strip, cut three 51½"-long sashing strips. Sew the block rows and long sashing strips together as shown. Press the seam allowances toward the sashing strips.

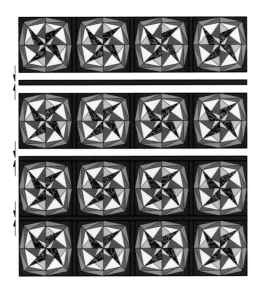

border. Press all seam allowances toward the just-added borders.

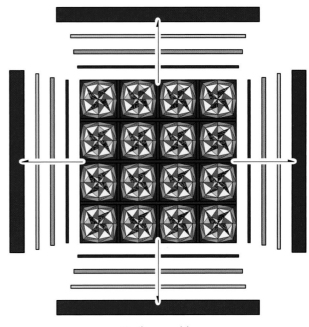

Quilt assembly

3. Sew the 1¼"-wide dark-purple strips together end to end. Refer to "Adding Borders" on page 11 to measure the length of the quilt top. From the pieced strip, cut two dark-purple strips to this length and sew them to the sides of the quilt top. Press the seam allowances toward the dark-purple border. Measure the width of the quilt top. From the remainder of the pieced strip, cut two dark-purple strips to this length and sew them to the top and bottom of the quilt top to complete the inner border. Press the seam allowances toward the dark-purple border.

4. In the same manner, sew the 1¾"-wide lavender strips together end to end and then measure, cut, and sew the strips to the quilt top for the second border. Sew the 1½"-wide gold strips together end to end; measure, cut, and sew the strips to the quilt top for the third border. Lastly, join the 5"-wide dark-purple strips end to end; measure, cut, and sew them to the quilt top for the fourth

Finishing

Cut and piece the backing fabric, and then layer the quilt top with batting and backing. After basting the layers together, hand or machine quilt as desired; see the quilting suggestion below. Trim the batting and backing so that the edges are even with the quilt top. Use the 2"-wide dark-purple strips to make and attach the binding.

Quilting suggestion

Unit A

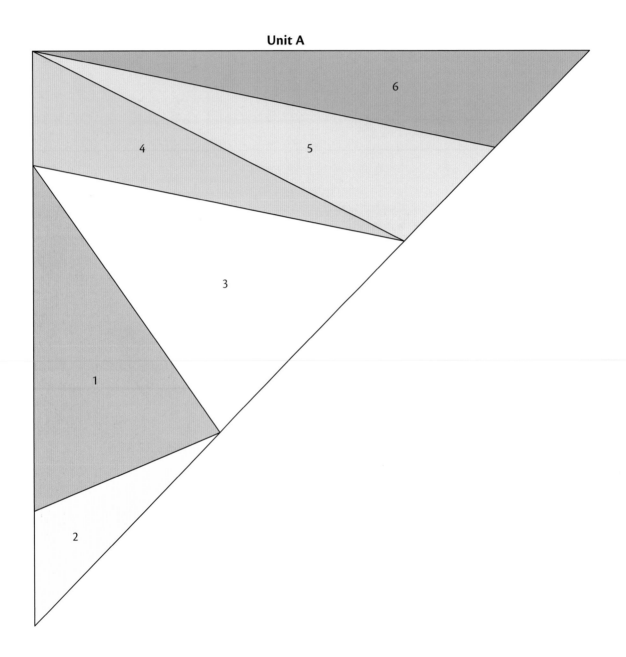

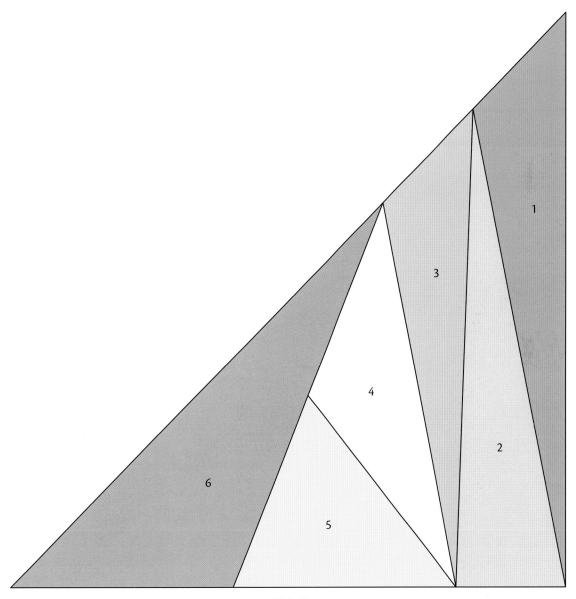

Unit B

Spring Green

Finished Quilt Size: 60½" x 60½" • Finished Block Size: 12" x 12"

Pieced and machine quilted by Nancy Mahoney

No matter what the calendar says, this quilt will bring a sense of spring into your home. Refreshing green fabrics create a soothing and restful atmosphere that can be enjoyed year-round.

Materials

Yardages are based on 42"-wide fabrics.

2¼ yards of black batik for blocks, fourth border, and binding

2 yards of cream batik for blocks and third border

1⅛ yards of beige batik for blocks and first border

⅞ yard of green #1 batik for blocks and second border

¾ yard of green #2 batik for blocks

½ yard of green #3 batik for blocks

½ yard of light-green batik for blocks

3¾ yards of fabric for backing

66" x 66" piece of batting

Foundation paper

Cutting

Cut all strips across the width of the fabric. You may want to cut a few strips of each fabric in each width, and then cut more strips as needed. Depending on how efficiently you use the strips, you may not need all the strips listed. For this quilt, I recommend precutting some of the pieces as described on page 7.

From the green batik #1, cut:
- 3 strips, 4½" x 42"
- 6 strips, 1¾" x 42"

From the cream batik, cut:
- 10 strips, 2¼" x 42"
- 7 strips, 4" x 42"
- 6 strips, 1¼" x 42"

From the light-green batik, cut:
- 4 strips, 2¾" x 42"

From the green batik #2, cut:
- 8 strips, 2¾" x 42"

From the beige batik, cut:
- 11 strips, 2½" x 42"
- 5 strips, 1¼" x 42"

From the green batik #3, cut:
- 3 strips, 3¾" x 42"

From the black batik, cut:
- 11 strips, 1½" x 42"
- 4 strips, 4" x 42"
- 7 strips, 3¾" x 42"
- 7 strips, 2" x 42"

Making the Blocks

1. Make 64 copies *each* of the unit A, B, and C foundation patterns on pages 64 and 65.

2. Refer to "Paper Piecing" on page 6 to paper piece 64 A units as follows:

    Piece 1: green #1 strips, 4½" wide (or use precut pieces)

    Pieces 2 and 3: cream strips, 2¼" wide

    Piece 4: light-green strips

    Pieces 5 and 6: green #2 strips (or use precut pieces)

Unit A.
Make 64.

3. Paper piece 64 B units as follows:
    Piece 1: beige strips, 2½" wide
    Piece 2: green #3 strips
    Piece 3: beige strips, 2½" wide

Unit B.
Make 64.

4. Paper piece 64 C units as follows:
    Piece 1: cream strips, 4" wide
    Pieces 2 and 3: black strips, 1½" wide
    Piece 4: black strips, 4" wide

Unit C.
Make 64.

5. Sew each A unit to a B unit as shown. Make 64 units. Press the seam allowances toward the B units.

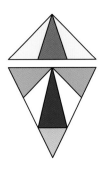
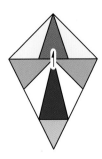

Make 64.

6. Sew a C unit to each A/B unit as shown to make a quarter unit. Make 64 units. Press the seam allowances open. Using a square ruler, trim any excess fabric along two sides as shown, making sure the center of each unit forms a 90° (right) angle and leaving ¼" beyond all points on the units for seam allowances. This little bit of trimming will make sewing the units together easier and help the blocks lie flat.

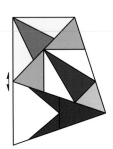
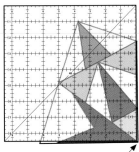

Trim excess fabric.

7. Arrange four quarter units from step 6 as shown. Sew the units together in pairs and press the seam allowances open. Sew the pairs together, matching the seam intersections. Press the seam allowances open. Make 16 blocks.

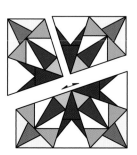
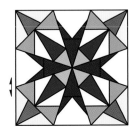

Make 16.

Assembling the Quilt Top

1. Lay out four rows of four blocks each as shown. Sew the blocks in each row together. Press the seam allowances in opposite directions from row to row. Sew the rows together and press the seam allowances in one direction.

2. Sew the 1¼"-wide beige strips together end to end. Refer to "Adding Borders" on page 11 to measure the length of the quilt top. From the pieced strip, cut two beige strips to this length and sew them to the sides of the quilt top. Press the seam allowances toward the beige border. Measure the width of the quilt top. From the remainder of the pieced strip, cut two beige strips to this length and sew them to the top and bottom of the quilt top to complete the inner border. Press the seam allowances toward the border.

3. In the same manner, sew the 1¾"-wide green #1 strips together end to end and then measure, cut, and sew the strips to the quilt top for the second border. Sew the 1¼"-wide cream strips together end to end; measure, cut, and sew the strips to the quilt top for the third border. Lastly, join the 3¾"-wide black strips end to end; measure, cut, and sew them to the quilt top for the fourth border.

Press all seam allowances toward the just-added borders.

Quilt assembly

Finishing

Cut and piece the backing fabric, and then layer the quilt top with batting and backing. After basting the layers together, hand or machine quilt as desired; see the quilting suggestion below. Trim the batting and backing so that the edges are even with the quilt top. Use the 2"-wide black strips to make and attach the binding.

Quilting suggestion

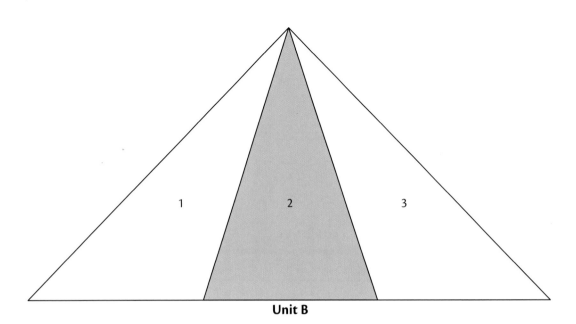

Unit B

Unit A

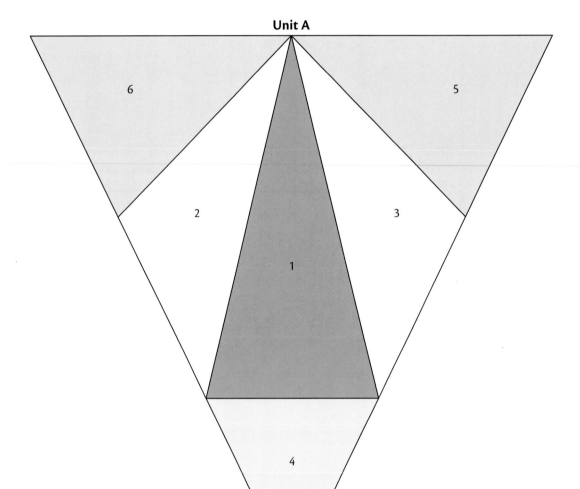

Unit C

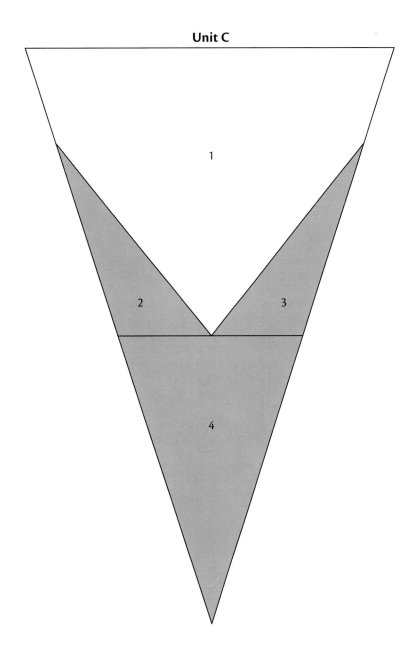

1

2   3

4

Spinning My Blues Away

Finished Quilt Size: 59" x 59" • Finished Block Size: 12" x 12"

Pieced and machine quilted by Mary DeWind

This mesmerizing quilt is sure to make you dizzy with delight. The more you look at it, the more you see! From the pinwheel design that forms in the middle of each block to the secondary design that forms when the blocks meet, this quilt is anything but glum.

Materials

Yardages are based on 42"-wide fabrics.

2⅞ yards of dark-blue batik #1 for blocks, outer border, and binding

¾ yard of dark-blue batik #2 for blocks

½ yard of dark-blue batik #3 for blocks

1⅜ yards of cream batik for blocks

1¼ yards of brown batik for blocks

1 yard of gold batik for blocks and inner border

1 yard of light-blue batik for blocks

⅞ yard of medium-blue batik for blocks

¾ yard of lilac-dots batik for blocks

½ yard of sky-blue batik for blocks

3¾ yards of fabric for backing

65" x 65" piece of batting

Foundation paper

Cutting

Cut all strips across the width of the fabric. You may want to cut a few strips in each width, and then cut more strips as you need them. Depending on how efficiently you use the strips, you may not need all the strips listed.

From the brown batik, cut:
- 13 strips, 3" x 42"

From the cream batik, cut:
- 19 strips, 2¼" x 42"

From the medium-blue batik, cut:
- 13 strips, 2" x 42"

From the gold batik, cut:
- 15 strips, 1½" x 42"
- 5 strips, 1¼" x 42"

From the light-blue batik, cut:
- 15 strips, 1½" x 42"
- 3 strips, 2¼" x 42"

From the dark-blue batik #2, cut:
- 6 strips, 2" x 42"
- 7 strips, 1½" x 42"

From the lilac-dots batik, cut:
- 6 strips, 1½" x 42"
- 6 strips, 2¼" x 42"

From the dark-blue batik #3, cut:
- 8 strips, 1½" x 42"

From the sky-blue batik, cut:
- 8 strips, 1½" x 42"

From the dark-blue batik #1, cut:
- 3 strips, 2¼" x 42"
- 13 strips, 3" x 42"
- 6 strips, 5" x 42"
- 7 strips, 2" x 42"

Making the Blocks

1. Make 64 copies *each* of the unit A and B foundation patterns on pages 70 and 71.

2. Refer to "Paper Piecing" on page 6 to paper piece 64 A units as follows:

   Piece 1: brown strips

   Piece 2: cream strips

   Piece 3: medium-blue strips

   Piece 4: gold strips, 1½" wide

   Piece 5: light-blue strips, 1½" wide

   Piece 6: dark-blue #2 strips, 2" wide

   Piece 7: lilac-dots strips, 1½" wide

   Piece 8: dark-blue #3 strips

   Piece 9: sky-blue strips

   Piece 10: dark-blue #1 strips, 2¼" wide

Unit A.
Make 64.

3. Paper piece 64 B units as follows:

   Piece 1: light-blue strips, 2¼" wide

   Piece 2: dark-blue #3 strips

   Piece 3: sky-blue strips

   Piece 4: dark-blue #2 strips, 1½" wide

   Piece 5: lilac-dots strips, 2¼" wide

   Piece 6: gold strips, 1½" wide

   Piece 7: light-blue strips, 1½" wide

   Piece 8: medium-blue strips

   Piece 9: cream strips

   Piece 10: dark-blue #1 strips, 3" wide

Unit B.
Make 64.

4. Sew each A unit to a B unit as shown to make quarter units. Make 64 units. Press the seam allowances open. Using a square ruler, trim any excess fabric along two sides as shown, making sure the center of each unit forms a 90° (right) angle and leaving ¼" beyond all points on the units for seam allowances. This little bit of trimming will make sewing the units together easier and help the blocks lie flat.

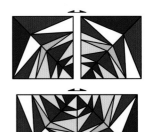

Make 64.   Trim excess fabric.

5. Arrange four quarter units from step 4 as shown. Sew the units together in pairs and press the seam allowances open. Sew the pairs together, matching the seam intersections. Press the seam allowances open. Make 16 blocks.

Make 16.

Assembling the Quilt Top

1. Lay out four rows of four blocks each as shown. Sew the blocks in each row together. Press the seam allowances in opposite directions from row to row. Sew the rows together and press the seam allowances in one direction.

2. Sew the 1¼"-wide gold strips together end to end. Refer to "Adding Borders" on page 11 to measure the length of the quilt top. From the pieced strip, cut two gold strips to this length and sew them to the sides of the quilt top. Press the seam allowances toward the gold border. Measure the width of the quilt top. From the remainder of the pieced strip, cut two gold strips to this length and sew them to the top and bottom of the quilt top to complete the inner border. Press the seam allowances toward the border.

3. In the same manner, sew the 5"-wide dark-blue #1 strips end to end; measure, cut, and sew them to the quilt top for the outer border. Press all seam allowances toward the just-added borders.

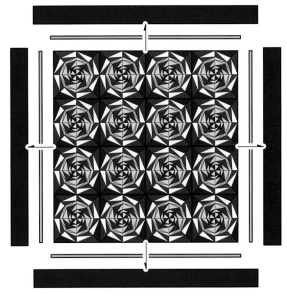

Quilt assembly

Finishing

Cut and piece the backing fabric, and then layer the quilt top with batting and backing. After basting the layers together, hand or machine quilt as desired; see the quilting suggestion below. Trim the batting and backing so that the edges are even with the quilt top. Use the 2"-wide dark-blue #1 strips to make and attach the binding.

Quilting suggestion

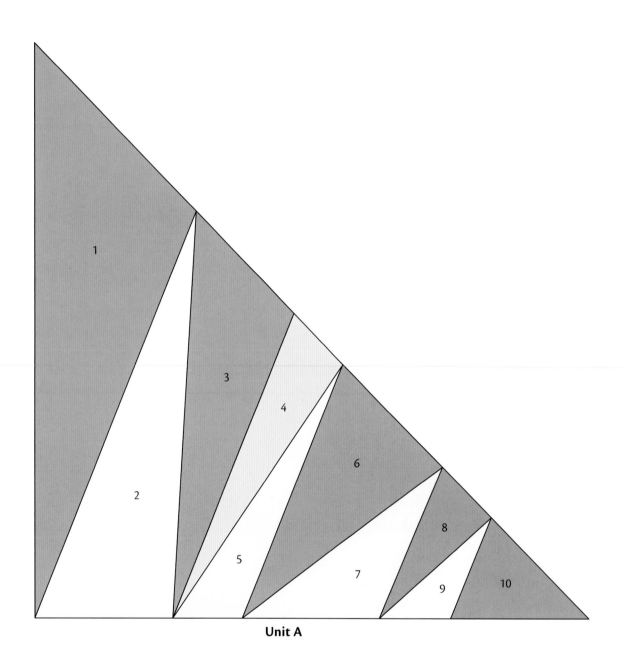

Unit A

Unit B

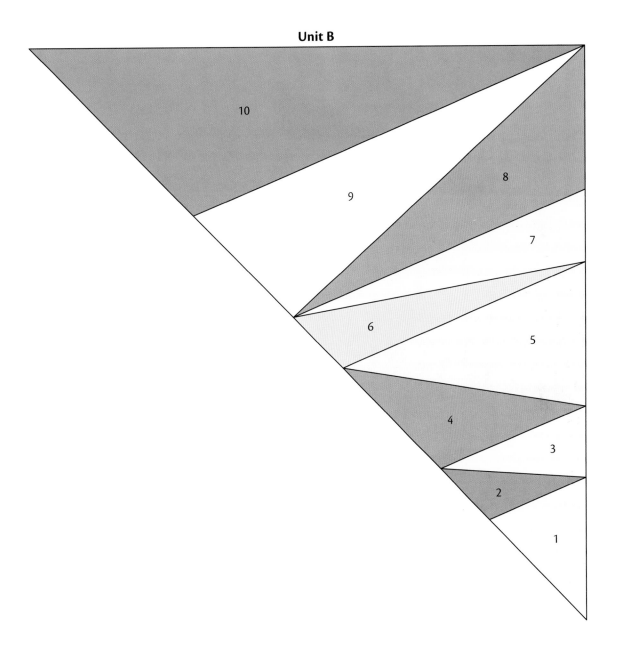

Raspberry Truffle

Finished Quilt Size: 57¾" x 57¾" • Finished Block Size: 12" x 12"

Pieced and machine quilted by Nancy Mahoney

A fantastic combination of black-and-white dots and a terrific stripe set the stage for this fun quilt. Add a scrappy, funky border, and your heart will sing with delight as you dream of dark chocolate and raspberries.

Materials

Yardages are based on 42"-wide fabrics.

2¾ yards *total* of assorted black, white, and red fabrics for pieced border

1¼ yards of white-on-white fabric for blocks

1¼ yards of black-with-white dots fabric for inner border, outer border, and binding

1 yard of red fabric #1 for blocks and sashing

¼ yard of red fabric #2 for blocks

⅜ yard of red fabric #3 for blocks

⅞ yard of black-and-white striped fabric for blocks

⅝ yard of white-with-black dots fabric for sashing

⅝ yard of black-with-circles fabric for blocks and sashing squares

⅝ yard of dark-red fabric for blocks

⅜ yard of black tone-on-tone fabric for blocks

3¾ yards of fabric for backing

65" x 65" piece of batting

Foundation paper

Cutting

Cut all strips across the width of the fabric. You may want to cut a few strips in each width, and then cut more strips as you need them. Depending on how efficiently you use the strips, you may not need all the strips listed. For this quilt, I recommend precutting some of the pieces as described on page 7.

From the red fabric #1, cut:
- 5 strips, 2¼" x 42"; crosscut into 72 rectangles, 2¼" x 2½"
- 16 strips, 1⅛" x 42"

From the black tone-on-tone fabric, cut:
- 9 strips, 1" x 42"

From the red fabric #2, cut:
- 3 strips, 2" x 42"

From the white-on-white fabric, cut:
- 8 strips, 2" x 42"
- 12 strips, 1¾" x 42"

From the black-with-circles fabric, cut:
- 9 strips, 1¾" x 42"
- 1 strip, 2⅜" x 42"; crosscut into 16 squares, 2⅜" x 2⅜"

From the dark-red fabric, cut:
- 9 strips, 1¾" x 42"

From the red fabric #3, cut:
- 6 strips, 1¾" x 42"

From the black-and-white striped fabric, cut:
- 15 strips, 1¾" x 42"

From the white-with-black dots fabric, cut:
- 8 strips, 1⅛" x 42"

From the black-with-white dots fabric, cut:
- 5 strips, 1⅝" x 42"
- 6 strips, 2¼" x 42"
- 7 strips, 2" x 42"

From the assorted black, white, and red fabrics, cut a *total* of:
- 39 strips, 2" x 42"

From the remainder of the assorted black fabrics, cut a *total* of:
- 8 rectangles, 2½" x 5½"

Making the Blocks

1. Using the foundation patterns on page 77, make 72 copies of unit A and 36 copies *each* of units B and C.

2. Refer to "Paper Piecing" on page 6 to paper piece 72 A units as follows:

   Piece 1: red #1 rectangle

   Pieces 2 and 3: black tone-on-tone strips

   Piece 4: red #2 strips

   Pieces 5 and 6: white-on-white strips, 2" wide

   Piece 7: black-with-circles strips (or use precut pieces)

   Piece 8: dark-red strips

   Pieces 9 and 10: white-on-white strips, 1¾" wide (or use precut pieces)

Unit A.
Make 72.

3. Paper piece 36 B units as follows:

   Piece 1: red #3 strips

   Piece 2: black-and-white striped strips

Unit B.
Make 36.

4. Paper piece 36 C units as follows:

   Piece 1: black-and-white striped strips

   Piece 2: red #3 strips

Unit C.
Make 36.

5. Sew a B unit to 36 of the A units as shown. Press the seam allowances open. Sew a C unit to the remaining 36 A units and press the seam allowances open.

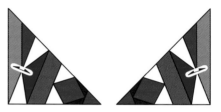

Make 36 of each.

6. Sew an A/B unit to an A/C unit as shown to make a quarter unit. Make 36 units. Using a square ruler, trim any excess fabric along two sides as shown, making sure the center of each unit forms a 90° (right) angle and leaving ¼" beyond all points on the units for seam allowances. This little bit of trimming will make sewing the units together easier and help the blocks lie flat.

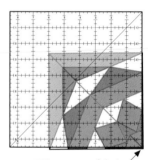

Make 36.   Trim excess fabric.

7. Arrange four quarter units from step 6 as shown. Sew the units together in pairs and press the seam allowances open. Sew the pairs together, matching the seam intersections. Press the seam allowances open. Make nine blocks.

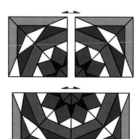

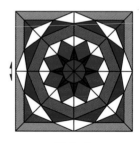

Make 9.

Making the Pieced Border

1. Using the foundation patterns on pages 78 and 79, make 24 copies of the border unit and four copies of the corner unit.

2. Refer to "Paper Piecing" to paper piece 24 border units, randomly using the 2"-wide assorted black, white, and red strips.

Border unit.
Make 24.

3. Paper piece four corner units as follows:
   Piece 1: assorted black rectangles
   Piece 2: assorted white strips
   Piece 3: assorted red strips
   Piece 4: assorted white strips
   Piece 5: assorted black rectangles

Corner unit.
Make 4.

4. Sew six border units together as shown to make a border strip. Press the seam allowances in one direction. The border strip should measure 46¼" long. Make four border strips.

Make 4.

Assembling the Quilt Top

1. Join two 1⅛" red #1 strips and one white-with-black dots strip together along their long edges. Press the seam allowances toward the red strips. Make a total of eight strip sets. Crosscut the strip sets into 24 segments, 12½" wide.

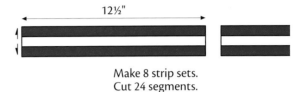

Make 8 strip sets.
Cut 24 segments.

2. Lay out four segments from step 1 and three blocks as shown. Sew the pieces together to make a block row, pressing the seam allowances toward the sashing strips. Make a total of three block rows.

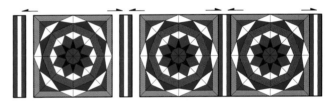

Make 3.

3. Lay out four 2⅜" black-with-circles squares and three segments from step 1 as shown. Sew the pieces together to make a sashing row, pressing the seam allowances toward the sashing strips. Make a total of four sashing rows.

Make 4.

4. Sew the block rows and sashing rows together, alternating them as shown. Press the seam allowances toward the sashing rows. The quilt top should measure 44" square.

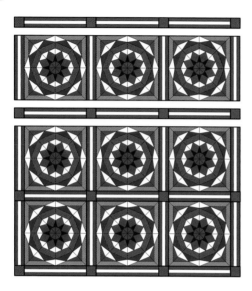

5. Sew the 1⅝"-wide black-with-white dots strips together end to end. From the pieced strip, cut two 44"-long strips and sew them to the sides of the quilt top. Press the seam allowances toward the black border. From the remainder of the pieced strip, cut two 46¼"-long strips and sew them to the top and bottom of the quilt top to complete the inner border. Press the seam allowances toward the black border. The quilt top should measure 46¼" square.

6. Sew two pieced borders to opposite sides of the quilt top and press the seam allowances toward the inner border. Sew a corner unit to each end of the remaining two pieced borders as shown in the quilt assembly diagram and press the seam allowances toward the borders. Sew the borders to the top and bottom of the quilt top and press the seam allowances toward the inner borders.

7. Sew the 2¼"-wide black-with-white dots strips together end to end. Refer to "Adding Borders" on page 11 to measure the length of the quilt top. From the pieced strip, cut two strips to this length and sew them to the sides of the quilt top. Press the seam allowances toward the outer border.

Measure the width of the quilt top. From the remainder of the pieced strip, cut two strips to this length and sew them to the top and bottom of the quilt top for the outer border. Press the seam allowances toward the outer border.

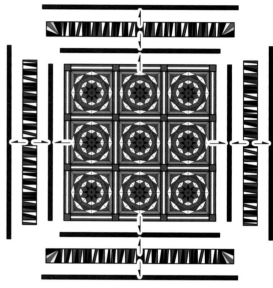

Quilt assembly

Finishing

Cut and piece the backing fabric, and then layer the quilt top with batting and backing. After basting the layers together, hand or machine quilt as desired; see the quilting suggestion below. Trim the batting and backing so that the edges are even with the quilt top. Use the 2"-wide black-with-white dots strips to make and attach the binding.

Quilting suggestion

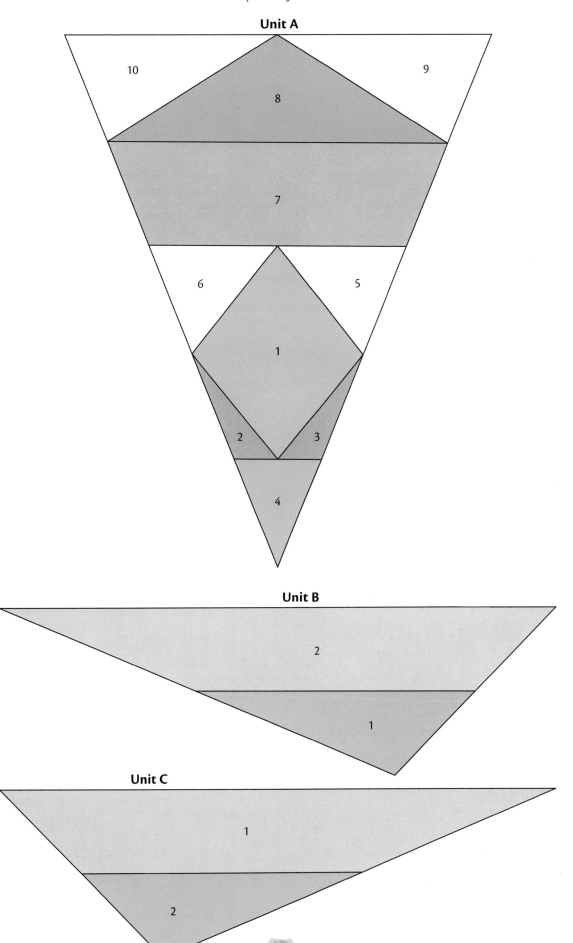

Unit A

10

9

8

7

6

5

1

2

3

4

Unit B

2

1

Unit C

1

2

Border unit

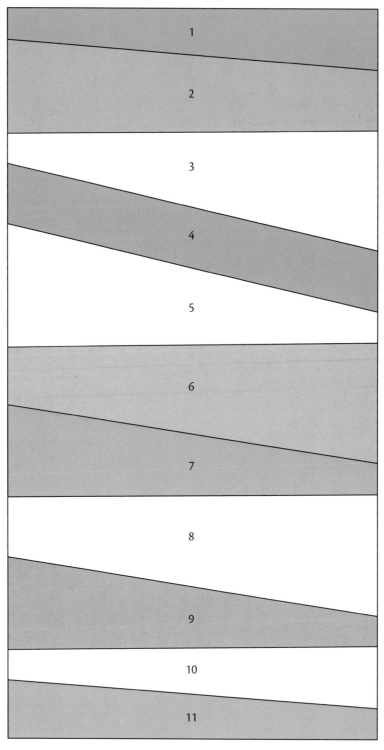

Corner unit

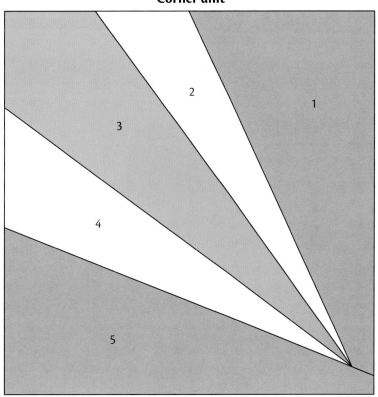

Acknowledgments

Many people will walk in and out of your life, but only true friends will leave footprints in your heart.
Eleanor Roosevelt

There are quilting angels in my life, women who have jumped in and helped when I've needed it the most. Thank you, thank you to Elizabeth Allocco, Silvia Ciofalo, Mary DeWind, Dee Duckworth, and Gillian Smith. I owe you huge!

And thank you to my sister, Karen Hodge, and to Shirley Chambers for helping pull everything together to complete "Raspberry Truffle." Thank you hardly seems enough.

The Memory Makers Quilt Guild—a delightful group of women, whose enthusiasm always inspires me.

Tom Reichert, for giving me time to do what I love, even when it means that there is less time for other things. His never-ending support and encouragement make all things possible! And thank you for letting me turn the house into a sewing room!

The wonderful people at Martingale & Company; this team of dedicated women and men are always a joy to work with! Thank you for producing great books I can be proud of.

The following companies who generously provided so many great products: P&B Textiles and Timeless Treasures, whose lovely fabrics created the quilts; Sulky threads and adhesives; Fairfield, for their wonderful Soft Touch batting; and Prym Dritz, for their rulers and other exceptional products.

About the Author

Author, teacher, fabric designer, and award-winning quiltmaker, Nancy Mahoney has enjoyed making quilts for more than 25 years. An impressive range of her beautiful quilts have been featured in more than 100 national and international quilt magazines.

This is Nancy's twelfth book with Martingale & Company. Her other best-selling titles include *Fast, Fusible Flower Quilts* (2011), *Treasures from the '30s (2010)*, *Ribbon Star Quilts* (2008), and *Appliqué Quilt Revival* (2008).

When she's not designing and making quilts, Nancy enjoys traveling to guilds and events around the country, sharing her quilts, teaching her piecing and machine-appliqué techniques, and visiting gardens.

Nancy makes her home in Florida with her life partner of over 35 years, Tom, and their umbrella cockatoo, Prince.

There's More Online!
Please visit Nancy at www.nancymahoney.com.
Find additional terrific books on quilting, knitting, crochet, and more at www.martingale-pub.com.